ROADS TO MATURITY

VERS LA MATURITÉ

Proceedings of the Second Canadian Conference on Children

MONTRÉAL, OCTOBER 31–NOVEMBER 4, 1965

Délibérations de la second Conférence Canadienne de l'Enfance

ROADS TO MATURITY

VERS LA MATURITÉ

Edited by MARGERY KING

UNIVERSITY OF TORONTO PRESS

Reprinted 2017
ISBN 978-1-4875-9229-5 (paper)

Foreword

A CONFERENCE BASED PRIMARILY on discussion groups presents particular problems for those who are preparing the proceedings. So much of the essence of the conference is in the face-to-face confrontation and much of this process is inevitably lost in transmission. We believe we are fortunate, however, to have had Dr. Alan Thomas's report each morning to draw together the threads of the previous day's deliberations, and especially to have had the brilliant summary presented by Dr. J. F. McCreary on behalf of the Conclusions Committee.

The proceedings of the Conference consisted of these summaries, the formal papers presented by Dr. Alva Myrdal, Dr. Alan Ross, Dr. M. S. Rabinovitch, Professor C. E. Hendry, and the Very Reverend Roger Guindon, Rector of Ottawa University, and the history of the Conference presented by the President, Dr. Reva Gerstein.

A special word of appreciation for the success of the Conference must be paid to the discussion group leaders and to Mr. R. D. McDonald of Sir George Williams University, who organized and co-ordinated their efforts. Not only did the discussion leaders contribute their skill and understanding of the group process throughout the Conference, but they also spent two days before the Conference working together to ensure that the subject matter and aims of the Conference should also be familiar to them. We are greatly in their debt.

A word of special thanks is also due to the authors of the preparatory documents, not only for their work in advance but also for their participation at the time of the Conference.

We are also grateful to Mr. St. Clair Balfour and the members of the finance committee as well as to the governments, individuals, foundations, and business organizations who again provided financial assistance to the Conference. Without their help we could not have moved forward on what turned out to be an extremely successful Second Canadian Conference on Children.

Six weeks before the date on which the Conference was to begin its site had to be changed because of a strike in Québec City. This created many complications, but Mrs. T. H. Dunn and her committee who were responsible for making local arrangements met the challenge with skill and ingenuity.

A conference where the delegates are broken up into small groups and where no one is "speaking," presents some very special problems for press, radio, and television. For this reason, we are particularly grateful for the sympathetic and accurate coverage of the Conference organized so ably by Miss Pat Harrison.

Special thanks go also to Madame Solange Vouvé who prepared the French translations for our preparatory documents and the proceedings; and, of course, to the Conference staff, Dr. Margery R. King, and her secretary, Miss Velma Faulkner.

It would be impossible to thank individually all the members of the board and committees, the provincial committees, the preparatory study groups, and all the delegates, and yet, in a unique way, appreciation is due to all. The success of this Conference was determined by their participation—without a desire for and a dedication to the conference process it could not have occurred. As Dr. McCreary expressed it at the closing session, "I hope you have been proud to be a part of the Second Canadian Conference on Children."

K. S. Armstrong
Secretary

Avant-propos

Un congrès basé avant tout sur des groupes de discussion présente quelques problèmes quand on en vient à préparer le compte-rendu. Les échanges directs qui forment une si grande partie de l'essence même du congrès sont pratiquement intransmissibles. Nous avons eu la chance toutefois d'avoir chaque matin le rapport du Dr Alan Thomas, et surtout d'entendre le brillant exposé, le dernier jour, qu'a fait le Dr J. F. McCreary au nom du comité des conclusions.

Le compte-rendu du congrès consiste en ces exposés et en les conférences données par le Dr Alva Myrdal, le Dr Alan Ross, le Dr M. S. Rabinovitch, le Professeur C. E. Hendry et le Révérend Roger Guindon, recteur de l'université d'Ottawa, ainsi qu'en l'historique de la conférence présenté par le président, le Dr Reva Gerstein.

Nous voulons signaler le rôle joué dans le succès du congrès par les meneurs de groupes de discussion et par M. R. D. McDonald, de Sir George Williams University, qui a organisé et coordonné leurs efforts. Non seulement ces meneurs ont-ils contribué de leur talent et de leur connaissance du travail en groupe tout au cours du congrès, mais ils ont également passé les deux jours précédant le congrès à travailler ensemble pour s'assurer qu'ils étaient bien familiers avec le sujet et les buts du congrès. Nous leur devons beaucoup.

Un mot tout spécial de remerciement aux auteurs des rapports préparatoires, non seulement pour ces travaux mais encore pour avoir participé au congrès même.

Notre gratitude très vive s'adresse à M. St. Clair Balfour et aux membres du comité des finances, ainsi qu'aux gouvernements, individus, fondations et organismes du monde des affaires qui ont encore une fois aidé financièrement notre conférence. Sans leur aide, nous n'aurions pu avancer dans nos préparatifs de ce qui s'est révélé être une belle réussite, le second congrès de la Conférence canadienne de l'enfance.

Six semaines avant le début du congrès, il a fallu en changer le site, à cause d'une grève survenue à Québec. Ceci a créé d'innombrables complications, mais Mme T. H. Dunn et son comité d'organisation locale ont fait des prodiges d'ingéniosité et de compétence.

Un congrès dont les délégués sont répartis en petits groupes sans orateur désigné pose de réels problèmes aux journaux, à la radio et à la télévision. Nous en sommes d'autant plus reconnaissants à la presse favorable que nous ont réservée ces média grâce à l'organisation de Mlle Pat Harrison.

Nous tenons également à remercier Mme Solange Vouvé qui a traduit en français les travaux préparatoires et le compte-rendu ainsi, bien entendu, que le personnel de la conférence, le Dr Margery R. King et sa secrétaire, Mlle Velma Faulkner.

Il serait impossible de remercier, un par un, tous les membres du conseil d'administration et des comités, les groupes préparatoires et tous les délégués. Et pourtant tous ont droit à notre gratitude. Le succès du congrès dépendait de la participation de chacun. Sans le volonté de tous de participer, il aurait été impossible de réussir. Et, comme l'a dit le Dr McCreary lors de la session de clôture : « J'espère que vous êtres fiers d'avoir pris part au second congrès de la Conférence canadienne de l'enfance ».

K. S. Armstrong
Secrétaire

Prologue

The Second Canadian Conference on Children was held at the Sheraton-Mount Royal Hotel in Montréal from October 31 to November 4, 1965. Its theme was "Roads to Maturity." This conference provided a very important forum where professional and lay people could come together to share their insights and to increase their understanding of children and youth.

There were about four hundred and fifty delegates from all parts of Canada. They represented the provincial committees of the Conference or one of some sixty national co-operating organizations which work on behalf of children. There were representatives of the federal government, representatives of industry who helped finance the Conference, and international guests. And, of course, there were the programme participants and the Conference planners.

The delegates to the Conference came together not to further their own professional goals but because of their concern for children. They came to this Conference also because they believe that many of the problems facing Canadian children cannot be solved by one individual, or one profession, or one organization working in isolation. They believe that only through team-work can adequate roads to maturity be opened for Canadian children.

In order to permit all delegates to participate in an experience designed to foster inter-personal and inter-professional communication, the major part of each day was spent in small discussion groups. There were twenty-five of these. Each day had a special topic: Monday—The basic issues; Tuesday—Why are there barriers? Wednesday—Finding New Approaches. The results of the previous day's discussions were summarized each morning and the conclusions were presented to the Conference on the closing day.

Our concerns about Canadian children were set into a world context by our keynote speaker who challenged us to look beyond our immediate social situation to the uniqueness in the development of each human being.

Because increased understanding and communication is difficult to assess, it is not easy to measure the success of a conference such as this. There were no "world shattering" pronouncements, no "scientific" discoveries. There was, however, an increased dedication to the importance of working co-operatively and an increased understanding of the part we each might play in opening roads to maturity for Canadian children.

Perhaps the words of one of the delegates best expresses the feeling of the participants: "The impact of this conference on the participants was well-nigh overwhelming. The exciting ideas which evolved from the discussions, and the somewhat startling recommendations which resulted could have far-reaching effects."

Prologue

LE SECOND CONGRÈS de la Conférence canadienne de l'enfance a eu lieu au Sheraton-Mont Royal à Montréal, du 31 octobre au 4 novembre 1965. Le thème choisi en était « Vers la Maturité ».

Ce congrès a permis de réunir un important forum où professionnels et profanes ont pu mettre en commun leurs idées et apprendre à mieux se comprendre dans l'intérêt de ce qui constitue leur majeure préoccupation, l'enfance et la jeunesse.

Il y a eu environ 450 délégués, de tous les coins du Canada. Ils sont venus représenter les comités provinciaux de la Conférence ou les soixante organismes associés qui se consacrent à l'enfance. Il y avait des représentants du gouvernement fédéral, des membres de l'industrie et des affaires qui ont aidé à financer le congrès, et des invités d'autres pays. Et, bien entendu, les organisateurs et les participants au programme.

Les délégués au congrès se sont réunis non pour servir leurs propres intérêts professionnels, mais à cause de leur intérêt envers l'enfance. Ils sont egalement venus parce qu'ils estiment que la plupart des problèmes touchant l'enfance canadienne ne peuvent être résolus par une personne, une profession, une organisation travaillant isolément. Ils estiment que seul un travail d'équipe peut ouvrir les voies de la maturité aux enfants canadiens.

Afin de permettre à tous les délégués de prendre part à une expérience destinée à faciliter les rapports interpersonnels et interprofessionnels, la majeure partie du congrès s'est composé de petits groupes de discussion. Il y en avait vingt-cinq. Leurs « tâches quotidiennes » ont été centrées : lundi, sur « les problèmes essentiels »; mardi, sur « pourquoi y-a-t-il des obstacles » ?; mercredi, sur « trouver de nouvelles méthodes ». Chaque matin étaient résumés les résultats des délibérations de la veille, et le dernier jour les conclusions ont été soumises au Congrès.

Notre préoccupation de l'enfance canadienne a été traduite dans un contexte mondial par notre premier orateur invité, le Dr Alva Myrdal, qui nous a requis de regarder au delà de notre situation sociale immédiate, et de considérer l'universalité du développement de tout être humain.

Il est difficile d'évaluer une augmentation dans la compréhension et les rapports humains; aussi est-il difficile d'évaluer le succès d'un tel congrès. Il n'y a eu aucun fait sensationnel, aucune découverte scientifique. Par contre on a senti accrue une prise de conscience de l'importance d'une étroite collaboration et d'une meilleure compréhension du rôle que nous pouvons tous jouer pour amener les enfants canadiens « vers la maturité ».

Le sentiment général s'exprime bien, nous semble-t-il, dans les mots d'un des délégués : « Le choc de ce congrès sur les délégués a vraiment été extraordinaire. Les idées passionnantes qui sont sorties des discussions et les conclusions parfois suprenantes qui en ont découlé pourraient bien avoir des résultats étonnants ».

Contents / Table des matières

History of the Second Canadian Conference on Children

DR. REVA GERSTEIN

The Canadian Conference on Children does not have a long history —but that, perhaps, makes its accomplishments all the more significant.

In 1956, largely through the impetus of Dr. Keith Armstrong and Mrs. J. D. Taylor, two groups of people started to meet in Toronto and Montréal. Their raison d'être was the belief that the problems faced by children and youth in Canada were such that they were not likely to be solved by any profession or special interest organization working alone. They believed that only by increased understanding between the professions, increased co-operation between organizations, could we possibly help Canadian children realize their full potential.

These two groups, working in partnership, planned a conference held at the Seaway Hotel, Toronto, in October 1957. Fifty-five people attended—mostly from central and western Canada. Their belief in the urgent necessity of a forum for inter-professional communication was so strengthened by the experience at the Seaway Conference that committees were formed immediately to plan for a meeting to be held in 1960 and to include delegates from all parts of Canada. I was asked to become Chairman of the Steering Committee and Dr. J. F. McCreary, then Professor of Pediatrics at the University of British Columbia, was named as Chairman of the Advisory Committee. In 1958 the organization was formalized and incorporated as the Canadian Conference on Children with Mr. Grant Glassco of Toronto as its first President.

From the beginning the Conference has been based on individuals —persons who, whatever their professional background or training, are committed to the idea that by learning to communicate we will be able to work together more effectively on behalf of children. Many organizations also wished to participate. They were invited to become "co-operating organizations" rather than sponsors. At present there are about sixty national organizations (see appendix for list) with whom we work closely and on whose support and co-operation we count.

In preparation for the first conference, provincial committees were formed and a series of studies undertaken to help us to assess "where we were" in the development of services in health, education, and welfare to meet the needs of Canadian children. Eighteen areas were chosen for investigation and the fourteen papers which were the result served as a background for the First Canadian Conference on Children held at Ste-Adèle and Ste-Marguerite, Québec, from October 2 to 6, 1960.

One of the objectives of the conference was to "provide a medium for better understanding among those engaged in children's work." The spirit of enthusiasm with which this aim was accomplished led to the decision that another conference should be held in 1965. In order to make this possible it was decided that we should establish a continuing national organization and that the provincial committees should be encouraged and assisted to maintain their identity and to continue their activities on behalf of children.

The next two years were largely devoted to re-organization. A new National Board of Directors and Advisory Committee were elected and many of the provincial committees were active, holding "reporting back" and "follow-up" conferences as a result of the Ste-Adèle meeting.

As early as 1962 the National Advisory Committee under the chairmanship of Dr. Alan Ross, Professor of Pediatrics at McGill University, began planning for this present conference. Recognizing that the documents from the Conference in 1960 provided primarily an analysis of the availability of services and programmes in the field of health, education, and welfare, it was decided that the next conference should direct its attention more towards the society which we have in Canada. Does it contribute to the development of maturity in Canadian children and youth? What are some of its strengths? What are some of its problems?

With this broad objective, the Advisory Committee decided on the theme "Roads to Maturity" and invited three sociologists to prepare papers which would point-up and summarize the evidence from research into the development of maturity in children and the social milieu provided for them in health, education, and welfare. The three resultant documents* supplemented by a fourth on Welfare Services, served as

*Details regarding these documents, which are available through the Conference Office will be found in the appendix, p. 125.

a basis for study before the Conference, within the groups organized by provincial committees and co-operating organizations. One thousand people or more were involved in the preparatory study groups and the deliberations of these groups have been reported through the central office and made available to each delegate to the Conference.

With this background preparation, we now come to this Conference. Delegates to it have all been specially invited on the recommendation of the National Board, the provincial committees or our sixty co-operating organizations. Most have been involved in preparatory study groups so we can truly say that "the Conference really started some time ago" and that our meeting together here is a high-point in an on-going process of inter-professional and inter-disciplinary communication.

In order to continue this process, delegates have been divided into twenty-five discussion groups each with a skilled leader.* The programme for the discussion groups has been organized and co-ordinated by Mr. R. D. McDonald of Sir George Williams University, Montreal. A link between one day's discussions and the next will be provided through the summaries undertaken by Dr. Alan Thomas, of the Canadian Association for Adult Education, and by the presentation of the areas to be considered each day. These presentations grow, in part, from the preparatory work for the Conference and are designed to focus discussion on different aspects of the theme, "Roads to Maturity."

Dr. Alan Ross, who has been Chairman of the committee that planned the Conference programme will present the "basic issues" to be considered in the development of maturity. Dr. M. S. Rabinovitch, Department of Psychology of McGill University in Montréal, will ask you to examine the "barriers or roadblocks to maturity" and Professor C. E. Hendry, Director of the School of Social Work of the University of Toronto will challenge you to find "New Approaches." The consensus or decisions reached by the discussion groups will be presented on the closing morning by Dr. J. F. McCreary, Chairman of the Conclusions Committee.

This conference has been organized to permit more than the usual amount of time for face-to-face participation by people in small groups. We not only talk teamwork, we have provided opportunities for the delegates to experience the understanding and appreciation that grows through a mutual attack on mutual problems.

At the First Canadian Conference on Children in 1960 Dr. Samuel R. Laycock, Chairman of the Summary Sessions, on the closing

*See appendix, p. 128.

morning said "I think you will agree with me that the amount of active and practical good-will and co-operation exhibited by the various professional, religious, racial, and regional groups has been outstanding at this Conference. There has been acceptance, understanding, and communication." It is the aim of this Conference to continually increase this acceptance, understanding, and communication. The Conference is based on the belief that together we can find new roads to maturity for Canadian children.

No history of the Conference would be complete without reference to another "act of faith": the financing of the Conference. Through the assistance of Mr. Grant Glassco and Mr. John Molson who organized and directed the financial campaign, the First Canadian Conference on Children raised all of its funds from private sources in Canada. It has been most encouraging for this Second Conference to receive government financial support not only nationally but also from eight of our ten provinces. The balance of the funds required for the organization of the Conference has been raised from foundations, business organizations, and interested individuals by the finance committee under the chairmanship of Mr. St. Clair Balfour.

The interest and support of such a wide section of influential Canadians lead us to believe that there is a partnership being developed between professional and lay persons which cannot help but benefit Canadian children and youth.

Historique du second congrès

L'HISTOIRE DE LA Conférence canadienne de l'enfance n'est pas encore très longue, mais cela fait ressortir d'autant mieux ce qu'elle a pu accomplir.

En 1956, grâce surtout à l'impulsion donnée par le Dr K. Armstrong et Mme J. D. Taylor, deux groupes commencèrent à se réunir, un à Toronto, un à Montréal. Leur raison d'être était leur opinion que les problèmes soulevés par l'enfance et la jeunesse au Canada ne pouvaient être résolus par une profession ou une organisation en particulier. Ces gens ont estimé que seules la compréhension et la collaboration sans cesse accrues entre organismes pourraient aider les enfants canadiens à développer pleinement leur potentiel.

Ces deux groupes, s'associant, ont organisé un congrès au Seaway Hotel de Toronto en octobre 1957. Cinquante-cinq personnes y ont participé, venant surtout de l'ouest et du centre du Canada. Cette expérience du Seaway a renforcé l'opinion qu'un forum inter-organisations était indispensable et on a aussitôt créé les comités nécessaires à l'organisation d'une rencontre nationale prévue pour 1960. On m'a prié de prendre la tête du comité des directives, et le Dr J. F. McCreary, alors professeur en pédiatrie à l'University of British Columbia a été nommé président du comité consultatif. En 1958 l'organisme devint officiel sous le titre de Conférence canadienne de l'enfance, avec, pour président, M. Grant Glassco, de Toronto.

Depuis le début, la conférence a été centrée sur les individus, des gens qui, peu importe leur profession, ou leur éducation, sont convaincus qu'en apprenant à communiquer ils pourront améliorer le sort des enfants avec plus d'efficacité. De nombreux organismes étaient également désireux de participer à la conférence, mais au lieu de se constituer garants de la conférence, ils sont devenus organismes associés. Il y a à l'heure actuelle une soixantaine d'organisations nationales (voir appendice) avec lesquelles nous travaillons en liaison étroite et sur le soutien et la collaboration desquelles nous comptons.

Pour préparer le premier congrès, nous avons formé des comités provinciaux et entrepris une série de travaux d'études pour mieux évaluer « où nous en étions » dans les domaines des services de santé, de bien-être et de l'éducation, et dans quelle mesure ces services répondaient aux besoins des enfants canadiens. On a choisi dix-huit sujets de recherches, avec, comme résultat, quatorze exposés qui ont servi de fond au premier congrès de la Conférence canadienne de l'enfance à Ste-Adèle et Ste-Marguerite, P.Q., du 2 au 6 octobre 1960.

Un des buts de la conférence était de « trouver un moyen d'établir une meilleure compréhension entre tous ceux qui se consacrent à l'enfance ». Devant l'enthousiasme qui a surgi de ce but, on a décidé de tenir un autre congrès en 1965. Afin d'y arriver, on a décidé d'établir un organisme national permanent et d'encourager et d'aider les comités provinciaux à conserver leur identité et à continuer de consacrer leurs efforts au bien-être de l'enfance.

Les deux années qui suivirent furent en grande partie consacrées à la réorganisation. Un nouveau conseil d'administration national et un comité national ont été élus et la plupart des comités provinciaux, très actifs, ont envoyé des compte-rendus et organisé des congrès pour étudier les conclusions de la rencontre de Ste-Adèle.

Dès 1962, le comité consultatif national, sous la présidence du Dr Alan

Ross, professeur en pédiatrie à McGill, a commencé d'organiser le présent congrès. Parce que les documents de 1960 nous fournissaient avant tout l'analyse de ce qui existait dans les domaines de l'éducation, de la santé et du bien-être, on a décidé que la prochaine conférence se consacrerait surtout à l'étude de la société canadienne telle qu'elle est. Contribue-t-elle à la maturation chez l'enfant et chez la jeunesse ? Quels sont ses forts et quels sont ses faibles ?

Avec ce but à l'esprit, le comité consultatif choisit comme thème « les chemins de la maturité » et pria trois sociologues de rédiger des essais qui mettraient en lumière et résumeraient les recherches sur le développement de la maturation chez les enfants et le milieu qui leur est offert dans les domaines de la santé, de l'éducation et du bien-être. Ces trois documents*, complétés par une étude sur les services du bien-être social, ont servi de base à des travaux préparatoires au congrès faits par des groupes d'études organisés par les comités provinciaux et les organismes associés. Au moins mille personnes ont participé à ces groupes d'études préparatoires, et leurs délibérations ont été transmises au bureau central et mises à la disposition de tous les délégués au congrès.

Voilà pour la préparation. Passons maintenant à ce congrés. Les délégués ont tous été invités personnellement sur les recommandations du conseil national, des comités provinciaux ou des soixante organismes associés. La plupart ont participé aux travaux préparatoires et nous pouvons vraiment dire que « la conférence a commencé il y a des mois », et que notre rencontre ici est le point culminant d'un travail continu de recherches et de communications inter-professionnelles.

Pour continuer ce travail, les délégués ont été répartis en 25 groupes de discussion qui ont chacun un meneur expérimenté†. Le programme de ces groupes de discussion a été préparé et coordonné par M. R. D. McDonald, de Sir George Williams University, à Montréal. Le lien entre les discussions d'une journée et celles du lendemain sera créé par le commentaire « au jour le jour » du Dr Alan Thomas, de l'Association canadienne pour l'éducation des adultes, et par la présentation des sujets mis à l'étude pour la journée. Ces présentations sont en partie le résultat du travail préparatoire au congrès et sont destinées à orienter les discussions sur les divers aspects du thème « vers la maturité ».

Le Dr Alan Ross, qui était président du comité d'organisation du programme, donnera une causerie sur les « problèmes essentiels » du

*Le détail de ces documents se trouve à l'appendice, p. 125.
†Voir appendice, p. 127.

développement de la maturité, le Dr M. S. Rabinovitch, de la faculté de psychologie de McGill University, vous priera de considérer « les obstacles à la maturité » et le professeur C. E. Hendry, directeur de la School of Social Work, University of Toronto, vous lancera un défi en vous priant de trouver de nouvelles méthodes. L'ensemble des conclusions auxquelles arriveront les groupes de discussion sera présenté le matin de la clôture du congrès par le Dr J. F. McCreary, président du comité des conclusions.

Ce congrès a été organisé pour permettre davantage de contacts directs et de participation par petits groupes. Nous ne faisons pas que parler de travail en équipe, nous cherchons également à donner la possibilité aux délégués de connaître la compréhension et l'appréciation qui naissent d'un travail en commun.

Lors du premier congrès de la Conférence canadienne de l'enfance, en 1960, le Dr Samuel R. Laycock, président du comité de récapitulation a déclaré avant la clôture : « Vous conviendrez que la bonne volonté, l'esprit de collaboration active, qui ont régné entre les groupes de professions, d'origines raciales, régionales, de religions différentes, ont été fantastiques. Grâce à la compréhension et aux communications, il y a vraiment eu acceptation les uns des autres ». C'est le but de ce congrès d'augmenter sans cesse cette acceptation, cette compréhension, ces communications. Le congrès est basé sur la conviction qu'ensemble il est possible de trouver de nouvelles voies vers la maturité pour l'enfance canadienne.

Un tel historique ne serait pas complet s'il ommettait un véritable « acte de foi », et je veux parler du financement de la conférence. Grâce à l'appui de M. Grant Glassco et de M. John Molson, qui ont organisé et mené la campagne de souscription, la première assemblée a pu obtenir les fonds nécessaires de sources privées. Ça a été un véritable encouragement pour ce second congrès que de recevoir une aide gouvernementale non seulement sur le plan fédéral mais, dans le cas de 8 provinces sur 10, sur le plan provincial. Le reste des fonds provient de fondations, du monde des affaires et de sources privées, et a été recueilli par le comité des finances sous la présidence de M. St. Clair Balfour. L'intérêt et l'appui d'un si grand nombre d'éminents Canadiens nous permettent de croire que l'association entre professionnels et profanes ne peut que servir la cause de l'enfance et de la jeunesse canadiennes.

INTRODUCTORY REMARKS

The Honourable Judy LaMarsh

I AM DELIGHTED to be with you tonight and to bring greetings from my colleagues in the Government of Canada and from the officials of the Department of National Health and Welfare.

We are all very gratified that the Second Canadian Conference on Children is now being held here in Montréal. It is a tribute to the success of the first conference in 1960 and it underlines the continuing need for the kind of voluntary initiative which was taken in arranging such a nationwide forum.

There can be no doubt of the ultimate objective of all of us who are engaged in fostering the well-being of Canadian children. These objectives have been spelled out forcibly in the draft declaration adopted by the United Nations Commission on Human Rights. In the words of that historic document, we are working towards the day when every child "shall be given the means necessary to enable him to develop physically, mentally, morally, spiritually and socially in a healthy and normal manner and in conditions of freedom and dignity."

That, then, is our ideal. It is reflected in the theme which you will be exploring over the next few days and the many significant steps which have already been taken to encourage younger Canadians along their roads to maturity.

Looking at the period which has elapsed since your last conference it seems to me you can find good reason for satisfaction in the continuing widening of opportunities which have been afforded to the young people of Canada. For example, there has been the implementation of the nationwide programme to promote fitness and amateur sports and the more recent introduction of a system of allowances to encourage school attendance beyond the age of sixteen.

There has also been increasing emphasis on, and a much more positive attitude towards, problems such as mental retardation. And I am particularly encouraged by the discussions at the national conference which was called by my department on the subject last

October. Moreover, the projected new system of medicare is bound to have profound effects in improving the availability of health care for children as well as for all other groups in our population.

Then, if you will permit me to do so, I should like to make an announcement in connection with Canada's Centennial year, which I believe will be of keen interest to all delegates to this Conference. I refer to the federal government's decision to include in its pavilion at Expo '67 a Children's Creative Centre. The Centre will be a major exhibit and will comprise a model nursery school, music, drama, and art studios and a nature playground complete with a tree-house, a canal with flowing water, a "real-life" grotto, and other fascinating features.

Staffing that Centre will be skilled teachers who will demonstrate the best in Canadian methods for stimulating imagination and for developing the creative potential of children from 3 to 11 years of age. The Centre will draw on children who visit Expo and will provide these youngsters with an opportunity not only to stretch their minds but to have fun. It will also serve as an exhibit of interest for parents, educators, and professionals engaged in children's work. I think the whole idea sounds wonderful and will be a real "feather in the cap" for Mrs. H. P. Hill who has worked with some fifty consulting experts in formulating plans for its design and operation. I know that we will all look forward to visiting the Centre and to the impact which it will have in stimulating and promoting that much needed new dimension in education—education for creativity.

In addition to bringing greetings from the federal government, I have the very pleasant duty tonight of introducing to you your keynote speaker for this Conference. This is especially gratifying because Dr. Alva Myrdal is one of the outstanding women of our times and also because it affords me the opportunity to renew a personal acquaintance which I value most highly. I shall never forget the very delightful occasion, on my first visit to Sweden some two or three years ago to discuss their pension plans, when Dr. Myrdal entertained me in her home at a reception. That meeting and the subsequent meetings I have had with her here in Canada are among the memorable experiences of my public life.

A sociologist by profession, Dr. Myrdal has held a long list of distinguished posts. After heading the Social-Pedagogic Seminary in Stockholm for 11 years she moved to the United Nations in 1947 where she served as director of a number of departments involved in social affairs. In 1955 Dr. Myrdal was appointed Swedish Ambassador to India, Burma, and Ceylon. Later she returned to the Ministry of Foreign Affairs in Stockholm where she became Ambassador-at-large with special responsibilities in matters relating to the United Nations.

Besides heading the Swedish delegation to the Disarmament Conference in Geneva, Dr. Myrdal has represented her government at meetings of the International Labour Organization and the United Nations Educational, Scientific, and Cultural Organization. Appointed to the Upper House of the Swedish Parliament in 1962, Dr. Myrdal is also a member of the Board of the Swedish Institute, the Dag Hammarskjold Foundation, and the Swedish government agency responsible for bilateral projects for aid to developing countries. Dr. Myrdal's activities are not limited to public service. She has been Vice-President of the International Federation of Business and Professional Women and has also found time to write and to collaborate on a number of important books in the field of sociology.

Of special interest to this Conference, I think, is the fact that as early as 1940, Dr. Myrdal forecast a social revolution which would attach new interest to productive investment in what she termed "a nation's chief economic asset—its children and their health and capabilities." In this context, Dr. Myrdal called for many of the measures such as family allowances which have since become important components of the social security structure of Canada and many other countries.

It is with this brilliant and varied background that our guest speaker comes to us this evening. Ladies and gentlemen I take great pleasure in welcoming to Canada and to your Conference one of the most charming and able women it has been my pleasure to meet, Dr. Alva Myrdal of Sweden.

ALLOCUTION D'OUVERTURE

L'honorable Judy LaMarsh

JE SUIS TRÈS HEUREUSE d'être parmi vous ce soir et de vous transmettre les salutations de mes collègues au gouvernement du Canada et des autorités de mon propre ministère, celui de la santé et du bien-être.

Nous sommes tous très satisfaits que ce deuxième congrès de la

Conférence canadienne de l'enfance ait lieu ici, à Montréal. Cela prouve le succès remporté par celui de 1960 et cela marque bien la nécessité d'un travail continu et bénévole tel qu'a nécessité l'organisation de ce forum à l'échelon national.

On ne peut douter du but poursuivi par tous ceux d'entre nous qui s'occupent activement de promouvoir le bien-être de l'enfance canadienne. Ces buts ont été décrits avec éloquence dans la déclaration de la Commission des droits de l'homme des Nations unies. Selon les termes de ce document historique, nous tentons d'arriver au jour où chaque enfant « bénéficiera des mesures nécessaires pour lui permettre de se développer physiquement, mentalement, moralement, spirituellement et socialement, de façon saine et normale, dans la liberté et dans la dignité ».

Voilà donc notre idéal. Il se trouve réfléchi dans le thème que vous avez choisi d'explorer pendant les jours qui viennent, et dans les mesures que vous avez déjà prises pour encourager les jeunes Canadiens qui empruntent les chemins de la maturité.

Si l'on considère la période qui s'étend entre vos deux congrès, il me semble que l'on peut s'estimer satisfait en voyant combien les possibilités offertes aux jeunes de notre pays se sont améliorées. Par exemple, on a mis en œuvre dans le pays tout entier un programme destiné au bien-être physique, un programme de sports, et l'on a récemment établi un système d'allocations destiné à encourager la prolongation de la scolarité au délà de la seizième année.

On a également attaché davantage d'importance au problème de l'arriération mentale, et on l'a envisagé de façon beaucoup plus positive. J'ai été très encouragée par le congrès national organisé par mon ministère sur ce sujet en octobre dernier. De plus, le système d'assurances médicales « Medicare » aura certainement d'importantes répercussions sur les services de santé mis à la disposition des enfants ainsi que des autres secteurs de notre population.

Et, si vous voulez bien me permettre de m'attarder sur le sujet de notre Centenaire, je veux vous annoncer ce soir une nouvelle qui, je pense, devrait intéresser tous les délégués à ce congrès. Je veux parler de la décision prise par le gouvernement fédéral d'inclure, dans son pavillon à l'Expo 67, un Centre de l'enfance créatrice. Le centre sera un des points d'intérêts les plus importants du pavillon ; il y aura une maternelle modèle, des studios de musique, de beaux-arts et d'art dramatique et un terrain de jeu en plein air avec maison dans les arbres, canal avec eau courante, grotte « véritable » et autres détails passionnants.

Le personnel attaché à ce centre comprendra des instituteurs de première classe qui démontreront les meilleures méthodes canadiennes destinées à stimuler l'imagination et développer la créativité des enfants de 3 à 11 ans. Le centre attirera les enfants qui visiteront l'Expo et permettra à ces jeunes non seulement de faire travailler leurs cerveaux mais de s'amuser aussi. Il servira aussi, nous l'espérons, à éveiller l'intérêt des parents, éducateurs et autres professionnels se consacrant à l'enfance. Il me semble que ce projet est tout simplement merveilleux, et que c'est tout à l'honneur de Mme P. H. Hill d'avoir travaillé en collaboration avec cinquante consultants pour préparer les plans de ce centre. Je suis sûre que tous nous avons hâte de visiter le centre et de nous rendre compte de l'impact qu'il aura sur le développement de cette nouvelle dimension de l'éducation, l'éducation pour la créativité.

En plus de vous transmettre les vœux du gouvernement fédéral, j'ai la tâche très agréable, ce soir, de vous présenter l'orateur chargé d'ouvrir le congrès. J'en suis tout particulièrement heureuse, parce que le Dr Alva Myrdal est une des femmes les plus remarquables de notre temps, et aussi parce que cela me donne la chance de renouer des liens de sympathie auxquels je tiens beaucoup. Je n'oublierai jamais comment, lors de ma première visite en Suède, il y a deux ou trois ans, pour discuter de la question des plans de retraite, le Dr Myrdal m'a reçue chez elle. Cette rencontre et les quelques autres qui ont suivi, ici au Canada, restent parmi les plus mémorables de mes expériences.

Le Dr Myrdal, qui est sociologue, a occupé toute une variété de postes importants. Après avoir dirigé pendant onze ans l'Institut socio-pédagogique de Stockholm, elle a dirigé un certain nombre de services aux Nations unies. En 1955, le Dr Myrdal a été nommée ambassadeur de Suède en Inde, à Burma et au Ceylan. Plus tard elle revint au Ministère des affaires étrangères à Stockholm en tant qu'ambassadeur sans poste, tout spécialement chargée de responsabilités auprès de Nations unies. En plus de diriger la délégation suédoise à la Conférence sur le désarmement à Genève, le Dr Myrdal a représenté son gouvernement lors de rencontres de l'Organisme international du travail et de l'UNESCO. Nommée au Sénat de Suède en 1962, le Dr Myrdal est également membre de l'Institut suédois, de la Fondation Dag Hammarskjold et de l'agence gouvernementale suédoise chargée de projets bilatéraux en vue d'aider les contrées sous-développées.

Le Dr Myrdal ne se consacre pas uniquement au bien public. Elle a été également vice-présidente de la Fédération internationale des femmes d'affaires et professionnelles et trouvé le temps d'écrire ou de collaborer à d'importants travaux dans le domaine de la sociologie.

Je pense qu'il intéressera tout particulièrement les assistants à ce congrès de savoir que dès 1940 le Dr Myrdal avait prévu une révolution sociale qui attribuerait un nouvel intérêt dans l'investissement productif dans ce qu'elle appelle « le principal capital économique d'une nation – ses enfants, leur santé, leurs capacités ». C'est dans ce contexte que le Dr Myrdal a réclamé un certain nombre de mesures telles que par exemple les allocations familiales qui sont depuis devenues un élément important de la sécurité sociale au Canada et ailleurs.

Tel est la brillante carrière de notre orateur invité de ce soir. Mesdames et Messieurs, je suis très heureuse d'accueillir au Canada et à votre congrès une des femmes les plus compétentes et les plus charmantes qu'il m'ait été donné de rencontrer, le Dr Alva Myrdal, de Suède.

ADDRESSES

DISCOURS

*Children of the World**

HER EXCELLENCY DR. ALVA MYRDAL

LET ME FIRST OF ALL say that it gives me great pride to be allowed to be with you today. I am truly grateful that you are welcoming me with such very warm words although I no longer belong in the field of specialization of this Conference. As Miss LaMarsh stated, my present duties have turned my main attention to very different problems, to efforts to prevent war, to preserve peace, that is to work for disarmament. It is nevertheless a special joy to be here and to share with you in the concern with children with which your country and mine are greatly involved in the nuclear age. Canada and Sweden are both in the fortunate position of being able to care, and to care very deeply, about children of the whole world, not just about those of our own nations. Representatives of our two countries have often met in international endeavours for the purpose of bettering the conditions of the children of the world. I think it must please us particularly today to know that the organ for which we have most persistently joined our efforts, UNICEF, has been selected to become a Nobel laureate for its services to that great humanitarian cause: relieving the plight of underprivileged children all over the world.

My keynote address is to be devoted to that very topic and I am consequently asking us all to take a global view of the problem of children's needs; I know that it requires much from our powers of imagination just as from our powers of compassion. As a matter of fact, it is probably easier to produce an echo of the latter in our hearts than it is to outline a coherent structure of knowledge in rational terms.

However, I am going to devote myself to the rational rather than the sentimental approach. In order to take a stand on the terra firma of reality, we must first recognize clearly what a cleavage exists in the world between rich countries and poor. It is a tragic fact that this rift between two different worlds should apply also to the children, so

*The Taylor Statten Memorial Lecture, 1965: the keynote address of the Second Canadian Conference on Children.

innocent of the long history of sins of omission and sins of commission of generations of masters, domestic or colonial. But in order to cope with this tragic situation, to remedy what is wrong and deficient, to help build a world of tomorrow for the young, we must start by accepting that the avenues of reform will have to be different ones. The methods we have used in our rich countries may not meet the needs in their lands.

Of course, I know that this is an over-simplification. But I need to make the statement about this cleavage of the world at the outset, as I could not cope with the topic given for my speech in one global perspective. I must be allowed to outline two quite different approaches, yes, even two different sets of objectives for our attempt to create a brighter future for the young of the world.

On one hand there are the children of the countries who have as yet remained poor, underdeveloped, underprivileged; they comprise four-fifths of all children. It is a gigantic undertaking even to assure satisfaction of basic needs, material and educational, for the children of the underprivileged parts of the world. For the remaining fifth, the children of the advanced countries, these basic needs no longer pose any real problems even though poor sections are to be found in all countries. Whatever is lacking in implementation, there is no uncertainty about our capacity to protect the needs of all our children as far as health and material well-being is concerned. We have just to proceed on the roads we have already outlined.

In our country, the problems occur in another direction, centring, as a matter of fact, much more around youth than around children. We have to face the challenge to adjust our whole social fabric to that new phenomenon of a considerably prolonged period when the young live in the twilight status of adolescence. The question is: "How can we provide an appropriate 'way of life' for the young adults in our midst?" I must emphasize the newness of this task: our civilization has never before faced the problem of having to cater for large groups of pre-productive adults. That is what they are: adults in the physical sense–splendid specimens of young manhood and womanhood–but youngsters in the social and economic sense, because they are dependents.

This is my diagnosis of the most poignant problems of children and youth. Consequently, I will review chiefly the problems of children in the poor countries and the problems of adolescents in the rich ones. It will also mean being more concerned with certain more elementary and material needs for the former, and with the societal needs of the ones who live right among us. Of course, in the real world the lines are not so clearly separated. The questions raised and perhaps also the answers proferred are intertwined. Thus, fortunately, the lessons we learn when trying to think straight about the problems of one group should benefit the other one also.

To you—distinguished conference delegates—who are professionals in various fields of social welfare it is most natural if the first problem fits in with your scheme of thinking: how best to satisfy the basic needs of the millions of children, hungry, sick, ill-clad, and ignorant. Your primary consideration must be methods for improving these conditions. Still, I may have to disappoint you, because I have come to believe that at present only in cases so rare as to be labelled exceptions, can the methods of planned social reform, of organized social welfare which have been tested in our countries, be applied in the underdeveloped countries.

The needs of their children, even if scaled down to bare essentials, cannot be met by any methods which involve in principle, as ours do, some system of income equalization, be it through taxation or through philanthropy, or by any method of social service which involves manning various agencies to care for individual families. The magnitude of the needs is so enormous compared with the assets in these countries, that they can only begin to be met if considerable progress is made to strengthen the whole economy of these countries. I do not want to turn my speech into a lecture on economics but the reminder must be raised that to be effective a remedy cannot concentrate on just one age-group but must call for gigantic strides forward along comprehensive national lines. It must affect agricultural production in order to provide food. It must increase all kinds of manufacturing in order to secure incomes from employment. This becomes self-evident if we just recall the simple fact that in those underdeveloped countries children constitute half the population or, to be somewhat more exact, something between forty and sixty per cent. That tells us, first and foremost, that in merely quantitative terms, the burden of providing fully for all children's needs becomes a nearly superhuman one. But it also tells us that as the children live right in the midst of the other half of the population, both halves will have to share progress. Measures, whether concerning food, shelter, or health, cannot be aimed only at children. A basic floor of security must be laid in these countries as a whole.

Take as an example the eradication of what is probably the primary cause of children's ill health and mortality. It is spelled out by the

World Health Organization in the simple word "dirt." To me—and I have no pretensions to be an expert but just a world citizen with an uneasy conscience and an eager curiosity about the real causes and real effects of the ills of the world—this is new knowledge, a re-emphasis of such simple essentials that I had comfortably forgotten them. In its more recent studies WHO has emphasized that "dirt," that is, unsanitary conditions, takes first place as a killer of children, while under-nutrition and malnutrition—despite its omnipresence—"only" takes second place. I would recommend some studies like that as primers in our own public schools so that our children would know what life can be like in other homes around this world. We have a handy reference book in UNICEF's recent study entitled *The Needs of Children*, published in 1963, where the contribution made by WHO is a particularly telling one. I will quote or paraphrase a couple of their findings.

Enormous differences in infant mortality rates are found in different parts of the world, from 500 per thousand live births in primitive and poverty-stricken countries to 15 in some developed countries with efficient health and social services. Under-nutrition and malnutrition are among the causes of infant mortality, but probably take second place to dirt, using this term to denote unsanitary conditions. This is because the infant's nutritional needs are usually fulfilled by mother's milk, while the dramatic fall in infant mortality rates which follows the introduction of simple hygienic measures indicates the importance of the sanitary factor. For these reasons the infant mortality rate cannot be considered a direct index of the nutritional status of a population.

More suggestive is the death rate in children aged one to four, the age group in which malnutrition is most common and severe. In the developed countries this is nowadays one of the safest periods of life. Figures from Sweden will illustrate this point. In that country the infant mortality rate—the number of deaths per thousand live births in the first year—is about eighteen. In the age group one to four the death rate per 1,000 population of the same age is about 1.0; that is, about six per cent of the infant mortality rate. If actual numbers of deaths are taken we find that in 1957 in Sweden 2,033 infants and 403 children aged one to four died. The Swedish figures are exceptionally good, but other highly developed countries can produce figures of approximately the same kind.

In the under-developed countries the picture is altogether different. The infant mortality rate will, of course, be higher; 100 per 1,000 live births may be taken as a typical figure. The death rate in the group one to four per 1,000 population of that age may be of the order of 20 to 60, or even higher. Suppose 40 is taken as a typical figure. This means that, typically, the death rate in the group one to four is 40 per cent of the infant mortality rate—in spite of the fact that the infant mortality rate is itself very high. In part of an Asian country in 1954 there were 687,082 infant deaths and

569,984 deaths in the "toddler" group. Parallel figures for one country in the Near East are 130,430 and 128,290 and for one Latin American country 28,348 and 19,087.

Such figures, however provisional, bring out a fact which is still insufficiently recognized: that children in the under-developed countries survive the first year of life only to enter into another dangerous period.

In short: dirt and malnutrition are the great slayers of children.

I am not going to fall for the temptation to quote page after page from the harassing findings about the actual plight of children living today in homes around the globe. But I want to underline the pertinent conclusion, that the living conditions of the whole population in the poor countries have to change if the lives of their children are to be changed. So I am back at the primordial challenge: agricultural production must be reformed, industrial production must be stepped up, the economic spiral must move upward.

If this does not occur where will the necessary food be obtained? As of today the countries with the greatest share of the world's child population are importing food from us, the rich countries: we run surpluses where they run deficits. Some of it is paid for—as is the case, I think, with most of the Canadian wheat exported—some of it is given away under one kind of aid programme or another, like the US PL 480 scheme. The international community is beginning to face the duty of keeping up a world food programme of considerable dimensions for some 20 years. But surely, such a situation cannot continue permanently, unless, of course, these countries produce on a large scale other goods for which there is a true demand in our countries in terms of hard and fast purchasing power.

This paradox persists, the paradox between poverty and riches. This imbalance between wants and resources is the dilemma in which the children of the world are caught. And do we not here agree that their suffering under this paradox is the most inhumane, the most intolerable, the most unpardonable feature of the times in which we live?

This amounts to a credo which social workers and socially minded people in all our countries must make theirs. There are no shortcuts to protecting the children if we cannot lift the whole country where the children live to a standard which we, in the twentieth century, can call a decent level of living.

Still, there are certain areas in which the fate of the children is of most particular importance. There are, to my mind, two, and perhaps not more than two, focal points on which a determined, even a militant effort by those who are specialists in child-welfare seems to be predominantly called for. I want to narrow the issues down for the sake of concentrated attention and ask you all to think of them and, in the future, if possible, to do something new and constructive about them: one is the enigma of what is called the population explosion; the other is the tremendous challenge of accelerating the process of development through the use of education.

Of course, I do not intend to give an essay on the socio-economic problem of population growth. We all know the outline of the population explosion process with the three billion figure for world population having been passed in 1960 and probably more than a doubling of it being foreseen for the end of the century—despite that rising spectre of hunger in every land. This is nothing less than a catastrophe of nature hitting our world. It now is the countries with large populations that are experiencing the effects of a discrepancy between birth rates and death rates which the smaller population groups in Europe went through a century ago. There, it produced what we used to call "the poverty decades" which we have long laid behind us and which, among other things, led to considerable emigration. Today, I would like to examine this situation in its more intimate context of the individual family. This was impressively done on the occasion of the World Population Conference in Rome, 1954, when the Pope made a statement to the effect that it was a responsibility of each family not to have more children than they could take good care of. As one who has been concerned with population problems for a very long time I think that this individualistic approach is the correct one to take in relation to the large poor regions in the world. It is the fate of the family that should be placed in focus, its health, the health of the mother and of the children already born, their chance for nourishment, care and well-being, rather than any abstract argument about family size and rate of population growth. If this is the line we choose, the avenue for reaching the family with birth control information also becomes indicated. The accent should be on spacing rather than on limiting births. The information about methods to achieve proper spacing must then be given from the time of the first pregnancy. The agency to give the information should preferably be the maternal and child health clinics that serve the family on prenatal and postnatal care and also midwives and doctors generally. In this way an unassailable chain for social action is established safeguarding the principle to which member nations have agreed, at WHO's latest World

Health Assembly, namely "that the size of the family should be the free choice of each individual family." A remarkable switch has been achieved during the last year or two in the publicly professed policies of the UN organizations with WHO, the Population Commission, and FAO now all favouring technical assistance in the family planning field. And UNICEF itself, at its board meeting last summer, decided—without taking a definite stand but in a positive rather than a negative vein—to include the question of UNICEF's role in family planning on the agenda of next year's session. The world does move—and it moves in such a way that perhaps it smiles with a hint of irony on us, the advanced countries. We are now faced with a situation in which the people of the poor countries want family limitation—any number of studies give supporting evidence—and in which their governments actually include family-planning activities in their plans and budgets, while in our own countries the corresponding movement has had to fight its way forward on the basis of private initiative, against the rather deadening hand of official inertia.

Controlling the population explosion is a must—for the sake of the children. This is one of the special considerations I am under a compulsion to urge alongside a general quickening of the economic process bringing less specific benefits.

The second plea which I must introduce is for a much more purposeful drive to use education as a means for improving the lot of the unfortunate continents, and most directly of their children, their next generation. I do not intend to bore you with statistics, because I know I do not need to in order to bring home my point. It is not news to you that in the poor countries the population is to a large extent illiterate, which means that the homes are full of stagnant ignorance. They lack channels to the pulsating civilization around them. This, of course, is an over-simplification: the figures vary between 4 per cent literacy for some countries like Nepal and Afghanistan and 66 per cent literacy in some other under-developed countries. Perhaps it is also too sombre. We might recall the fact that school enrolment for children has recently been rising conspicuously. Providing schools for their children has been one of the truly great ambitions of most countries as they become independent. UNESCO reminds us through its statistics that "some 90 million extra school places were provided" in the short period of 7 years in the 1950's. But—and here is the diabolical interconnection—because of the simultaneous growth in the child population the proportion of those being allowed to go to school has risen far less perceptibly; to use the same points of comparison, only from 10.2 to 12 per cent of the total population. Thus, the proportion of those without school opportunities remains dangerously static.

I wonder if we understand what this under-cultivation of the minds of the children means. It means that a majority of children are still growing up unable to profit from the fact that they belong to our century. To them life is probably very much the same as in the Middle Ages. We are losing every day thousands of youngsters who might have lived a different life. We are losing every year generations for the future who have not been equipped to live in a way that spells development. Having worked in, and paid visits to the three continents on the map of underdevelopment, I dare add that even those youngsters who can push their way into a school, are far too often fed on antiquated, undigestible pedagogical fare that does not open to them the vistas of modernization, nor provide them with the tools for breaking new paths of life—schools which, largely because of a too heavy heritage of Western patterns gives them what must be termed "mis-education," a Bapu education, an education for colonial hangers-on rather than for a free electorate and a competitive new economy.

I have felt a need to present what to my mind constitutes the two imperative challenges to us if we want to promote the well-being of children in the poor countries: the population explosion in store for them and the educational renaissance due to them. In comparison, special welfare schemes of housing, of adoption, of family allowances, yes, even of supplementary feeding and eradication of endemic diseases shrink in importance. You must first and foremost have a population of manageable size on which to practice new social devices and you must, through opening the channels of education, adult as much as, if not more than, that of children, set in motion their own forces to better their situation. And least of all should we overlook the fact that by introducing truly modern education, new attitudes in regard to health, to sanitation, to family planning, to productivity, we can create a cumulative process, a chain reaction where every step of progress multiplies and spreads. It is my sincere conviction that seen under the perspectives of world history, the richer countries could do no better than to start assistance on a grand scale for a world programme of aid to education, to school material, books, libraries, laboratories—all the expensive prerequisites for a stepped-up drive towards modernization.

This is all I can do to fulfil my function of provoking thought in regard to the lamentable situation of the great majority of the world's children.

But what then about problems closer to home? I intimated at the outset that all was not quiet on the Western front either. However, in comparing point by point the needs just reviewed for the underdeveloped countries with the corresponding situation in our own, we must conclude that the basic needs are met, that the main tasks are fulfilled as far as the children in the richer countries are concerned.

Of course, one can always point to loopholes in our social legislation, to the clamour for further extension of education, particularly for the pre-school years, to deepfelt needs for humanization of all forms of treatment and care of the physically, mentally, or socially handicapped. Lists of desiderata exist in our countries but they are so familiar to you already that there is no need to enumerate them in this brief survey of world problems. Besides, the waiting lists for such social reforms which mean adjustment and perfection read differently for each nation. We don't have to look long, however, before we discover one major problem, looming higher and higher on the list of social anxieties in all our countries. It is usually briefly denoted as the "youth problem"—which is a euphemism.

Everywhere we are surprised at the newness and sharpness of this problem, carrying different names depending on the various angles from which it is approached: juvenile delinquency, drunkenness, and drug addiction among the teenagers, sexual laxity, student indiscipline and intellectual restlessness, demonstrative untidiness and eccentric modes of dressing, a love for noisiness not without an undertone of aggressiveness, or the deadpan blankness of the crowds of youth roaming city streets. I am not going to analyse all the phenomena of social restiveness on the part of the young. Still less am I going to preach a sermon about them. We have only to state as a fact that our advanced societies have not succeeded in providing for a smooth transition from childhood to adulthood. We have failed to find a structural form for young people to move from dependence to independence in harmony with their own process of growth.

We do not look back nostalgically to the time when children were put to work before their backs were strong enough to bear the burden, but I do believe that our mental attitudes towards the periods in life are still shaped largely by the situation of some generations ago when, for the majority of children, the age for leaving school corresponded with the age for commencing employment—a fine harmonization of social rules against which we have all helped to legislate on the basis of the recommendations of the ILO. What our imagination has as yet not fully grasped is the effect of what I might call the "education explosion." I believe that in Canada 60 per cent of these below 20 are now in school, in Sweden we expect that in 10 years' time 70–80 per cent of the young between 16 and 20 will be in schools. This should demonstrate how our whole pattern of life is now changing, with predominant numbers of our population in training for the first two decades of their life. In simplified terms it means that age at which you have the legal right to marry and the right to vote is moving into the precincts of the educational period. At least the process of preparing for maturity in regard to these two extremely important events in human life—starting a family and participating in civic affairs—has now to be going on simultaneously with submission to school discipline and economic dependence.

This change to a considerably prolonged period of pre-productive life, reaching into biological, sexual, maturity without any corresponding change in our societies' institutional forms will no doubt appear startling to future historians. We who live through this period of swift social change have hardly begun to sense the challenge. To lament about the morals of the young is certainly no way to meet it.

I cannot here outline what is necessary for a constructive reorganization of our social forms and our personal ways of life. A whole new conference, or many, will be needed for the purpose. The adjustment of our socio-economic conditions has begun. Through the provision of free tuition, widespread scholarships, etc. partial economic coverage for the costs of being young is being established in welfare states. But where is it large enough to guarantee independence? Does it, even in the majority of cases, make it possible to set up comprehensive budgets which the young people manage for themselves? Through other practical arrangements—family apartments and nursery schools in the dormitories at our universities—the possibilities for students to marry and have a family are being increased. Still, I dare to doubt that this is a pattern which will be durable in the long run. When, for instance, at Uppsala University one-third of the students are now married, one cannot help but wonder whether many are rushing into marriage because this is a way, nearly the only acceptable way, to win a kind of freedom, of adulthood. Again it should be emphasized that I do not criticize. I only try to disentangle the social secrets behind a staggering new challenge and the kinds of half-way compromises made to meet it.

What is needed first and foremost is evidently a change in outlook. The very concept of the human life-cycle does not correspond to what it used to be. Adolescence is blending into adulthood under new conditions. And senescence is obviously being postponed with increased longevity or, at least, the social appearance and behaviour of older people is becoming more youthful. At both these crucial periods we need something more imaginative than just increased schooling for the young and retirement pensions for the old. Both of these age groups obviously call for a much more active and independent participation in life. For both, I believe the primordial necessity is to overcome the categorical cleavage between working years and the other years, the pre-productive and post-productive periods, respectively. They are too long, and far too empty of real meaning. For the young age group appropriate transitional patterns must in the future call for some form of life—perhaps of school, perhaps of camp—where productive, income-earning work is coupled with studies. Only by some such expedience might the other objective be achieved: a gradual relinquishing of parental supervision and authority—a relinquishing which is so rational to claim but in actual life so obstinately difficult to realize.

Finally, I leave the Conference the game of guessing which of the two problems the world will be able to cope with first. Will we find a way to protect the basic needs of millions of children in parts of the world which are too poor for them or will we first give to the younger generations in countries which have, nearly, given them everything else, a more independent, active, and respected role in a life which will consequently be more meaningful for them?

L'enfance dans le monde

PERMETTEZ-MOI D'ABORD de vous dire combien je suis heureuse et fière d'être parmi vous aujourd'hui. Je vous suis très reconnaissante de m'accueillir de façon aussi chaleureuse, bien que je n'appartienne plus aussi étroitement au domaine spécifique de votre congrès. Ainsi que Mlle LaMarsh vous l'a dit, mes fonctions actuelles consistent à m'occuper d'un problème très différent, celui de la prévention de la guerre, de la préservation de la paix, en un mot du problème du désarmement. Néanmoins ce mest une grande joie d'être ici et de m'associer à vos travaux sur l'enfance, l'enfance que votre pays comme le mien veut sauver et aider de toutes ses forces, même à l'âge atomique. Le Canada et la Suède ont tous deux la chance de pouvoir s'occuper vraiment des enfants du monde entier et non seulement des leurs. Des représentants de nos deux pays ont souvent collaboré dans des entreprises de caractère international visant à améliorer les conditions de vie de l'enfance dans le monde. Il me semble que nous devons nous réjouir tout particulièrement de savoir que l'organisme dans le cadre duquel nous avons si bien collaboré, l'UNICEF, a été choisi comme lauréat du prix Nobel pour services rendus à cette grande cause : le soulagement de la misère chez les enfants du monde entier.

Mon discours inaugural devant être consacré à ce sujet, je vais vous demander par conséquent d'envisager les besoins de l'enfance d'un point de vue global. Je sais que cela exige autant de votre imagination que de votre compassion. En fait, il est probablement plus facile de faire naître au fond de notre cœur cette compassion, que de tracer un tableau cohérent de nos connaissances en termes rationnels.

Mais je vais adopter l'attitude rationnelle de préférence à l'attitude sentimentale. Si nous voulons rester sur la terre ferme de la réalité, il nous faut d'abord reconnaître clairement quel abîme existe, dans le monde, entre pays riches et pays pauvres. Il est tragique que cet abîme puisse également exister quand il s'agit de l'enfance, innocente de la longue tradition de péchés par omission et par commission qui est celle des maîtres de ces pays, qu'il s'agisse de problèmes intérieurs ou extérieurs, c'est à dire des leurs ou des nôtres. Mais pour faire face à cette situation tragique, pour remédier à tout ce qui est déficient, il faut commencer par se faire à l'idée que les méthodes de réforme devront être différentes. Les méthodes que nous avons employées dans nos pays riches ne peuvent s'appliquer aux besoins de ces contrées.

Bien entendu, je sais que je simplifie énormément. Mais il me fallait vous parler de cet abîme dès le début, car il n'est pas possible de couvrir le sujet de mon exposé de façon unique et globale. Il faut que vous me permettiez de vous offrir deux perspectives très différentes, oui, et même deux types distincts de buts à viser dans nos efforts pour améliorer le sort de la jeunesse du monde.

D'un côté, nous avons les enfants des pays restés pauvres et sous-développés, et cela comprend les 4/5ièmes des enfants du monde entier. C'est une entreprise fantastique que de tenter de subvenir à leurs besoins élémentaires, matériels ou dans le domaine de l'éducation. En ce qui concerne le dernier cinquième, c'est à dire les enfants des pays évolués, ces problèmes essentiels n'existent plus, même si l'on trouve encore des secteurs de la population qui sont restés pauvres dans tous les pays. Même si les réalisations ne sont pas complètes, sans aucun doute nous pouvons protéger tous nos enfants, qu'il s'agisse de leur santé ou de leur bien-être en général. Il s'agit simplement d'avancer sur les chemins déjà tracés.

Dans nos pays, les problèmes sont d'une nature différente et concernent davantage la jeunesse que l'enfance. Il nous faut trouver un moyen d'adapter notre vie sociale au prolongement considérable de la période « crépusculaire » de l'adolescence. La question qui se pose alors est celle-ci : « Comment pouvons-nous donner un style de vie approprié à nos jeunes adultes ? » Il me faut insister sur la nouveauté du problème : jamais auparavant notre civilisation n'a du faire face au problème de s'occuper de groupes nombreux d'adultes au stage préproductif. Car c'est ce qu'ils sont : physiquement, de magnifiques spécimens d'humanité, mais des "jeunes" au sens économique et social du terme, parce qu'ils sont dépendants.

Voilà mon diagnostic des problèmes les plus poignants de l'enfance et de la jeunesse. Par conséquence, je vais étudier surtout les problèmes des enfants dans les pays pauvres et des adolescents dans les pays riches. Cela veut dire se pencher davantage sur les besoins matériels élémentaires des premiers, et sur les besoins sociaux de ceux qui vivent parmi nous. Bien entendu, dans la réalité, les frontières ne sont pas aussi marquées. Les questions – et peut-être aussi les réponses – sont entrelacées. Ainsi, par chance, les leçons apprises en tentant d'aider un groupe peuvent-elles servir pour l'autre.

Pour vous, délégués à ce congrès, professionnels distingués qui appartenez aux divers secteurs du bien-être social, il est tout naturel que la première série de problèmes rentre dans le cadre de vos préoccupations : comment satisfaire aux besoins élémentaires de millions d'enfants affamés, malades, mal vêtus et ignorants. Votre premier souci c'est de trouver les moyens d'améliorer leur sort. Je vais toutefois peut-être vous décevoir, parce que je finis par croire que ce n'est que dans des cas vraiment exceptionnels que nos méthodes de réforme sociale organisée, mises à l'épreuve dans nos pays, peuvent servir dans les pays sous-développés.

Les besoins de ces enfants, même si on ne s'attache qu'aux plus élémentaires, ne peuvent être satisfaits par des méthodes qui font entrer en principe, comme c'est le cas pour nous, un système quelconque d'alignement des revenus, par l'entremise d'impôts ou de philanthropie, ou par l'intermédiaire de services sociaux (ce qui veut dire plusieurs agences prenant soin d'une famille). L'ampleur des besoins est telle, comparée avec l'actif de ces pays, qu'on ne peut commencer d'y subvenir que si l'on arrive à raffermir et à consolider sérieusement l'économie nationale.

Je ne veux pas transformer mon exposé en cours d'économie politique, mais il faut tout de même se souvenir qu'aucune panacée ne peut être réservée à une catégorie d'individus déterminée par l'âge, mais qu'il faut avancer à pas de géant dans un contexte qui rassemble la nation tout entière. Il faut penser à l'agriculture pour améliorer et augmenter l'alimentation, il faut intensifier l'industrie dans tous les secteurs pour pouvoir distribuer des emplois et par conséquent assurer des revenus. Ceci devient clairement évident lorsqu'on se rappelle que dans les pays sous-développés les enfants représentent la moitié de la population (ou plus précisément, de 40 pour cent à 60 pour cent de la population). Voilà qui nous apprend tout de suite qu'en termes quantitatifs, suppléer aux besoins de tous ces enfants devient une tâche quasi surhumaine. Mais cela nous apprend aussi que, puisque les enfants vivent parmi l'autre moitié de la population, c'est l'ensemble qui doit bénéficier du progrès. Qu'il s'agisse d'alimentation, de logement, de santé, on ne peut réserver le progrès seulement aux enfants. Il faut un élément général de sécurité qui serve de base à tout progrès dans ces pays.

Prenez par exemple l'élimination de ce qui est sans aucun doute la cause la plus répandue de maladie et de mortalité infantile. L'OMS la traduit par un mot bien simple : *la saleté*. Pour moi – et je n'ai pas la prétention d'être un expert, mais seulement un citoyen du monde qui à la conscience mal à l'aise et qui éprouve une curiosité intense à l'égard des causes et des effets réels des maux de ce monde – c'est là une idée nouvelle, une emphase nouvelle donnée à des faits si simples que je les avais complètement oubliés. Dans ses récents travaux d'étude, l'OMS insiste sur le fait que c'est avant tout la saleté, c'est à dire le manque d'hygiène, qui tue les enfants tandis que la faim ou une alimentation malavisée n'a « que » la deuxième place. Je voudrais que nos écoles primaires se servent de ces textes comme manuels, pour que nos enfants apprennent ce que c'est que la vie dans d'autres parties du monde. Nous possédons des documents précieux sous la forme d'une étude publiée en 1963 par l'UNICEF sous le titre *The needs of children*, et dans lequel la contribution de l'OMS est particulièrement significative. Je vous citerai, ou paraphraserai, quelques-unes de leurs observations.

On constate d'énormes différences dans les taux de mortalité infantile dans les différentes parties du monde, de 500 sur mille naissances d'enfants vivants dans les pays primitifs, jusqu'à 15 dans certains pays où les services sociaux et sanitaires sont particulièrement efficaces. Le manque de nourriture, une piètre alimentation sont aussi parmi les causes de mortalité infantile, mais ne viennent qu'après la saleté, et par là nous voulons dire le manque d'hygiène. Et cela parce que les besoins alimentaires du bébé sont en général comblés par le lait de la mère, tandis que l'abaissement remarquable du taux de mortalité qui se produit dès qu'on adopte quelques mesures élémentaires d'hygiène, montre bien l'importance de ce facteur. C'est pour cela que le taux de mortalité du nourrisson ne peut servir d'indice à la condition de l'alimentation d'une population.

Plus suggestif est le taux de mortalité chez les enfants âgés de 1 à 4 ans, parmi lesquels la malnutrition est la plus fréquente et la plus sérieuse. Dans les pays évolués c'est là un des âges les moins exposés. Des chiffres pris en Suède l'illustrent clairement : dans ce pays, le taux de mortalité du nourrisson – soit le nombre de morts par mille naissances d'enfants vivants, au cours de la première année – est d'environ 18. Pour les enfants de 1 à 4 ans, le taux est d'environ 1.0, soit environ 6 pour cent du taux de mortalité du nourrisson. Si l'on consulte les chiffres exacts, on s'aperçoit qu'en Suède, en 1957, 2,033 nourrissons et 403 enfants de là quatre ans sont morts. Ces chiffres sont exceptionnellement bas, mais on en trouve d'équivalents dans certains autres pays modernes.

Dans les pays sous-développés, il en va tout autrement. Le taux de mortalité du nourrisson est évidemment plus haut, 100 pour mille est une proportion fréquente. Le taux de mortalité des enfants de 1 à 4 ans peut être de 20 à 60 par mille, ou même davantage. Prenons une moyenne de 40 : cela veut dire qu'en moyenne, le taux de mortalité des enfants de 1 à 4 ans est environ 40 pour cent du taux de mortalité du nourrisson, en dépit du fait que ce taux même est très élevé. Dans une région d'un pays d'Asie, en 1954, il y a eu 687,082 morts chez les bébés, et 569,989 chez les très jeunes enfants. Des chiffres correspondants sont, pour le Proche-Orient, 130,430 et 128,290, et pour un pays d'Amérique latine, 28,348 et 19,087.

De tels chiffres, même s'ils ne sont pas définitifs, font bien ressortir un fait, jusqu'ici trop mal connu, à savoir que les enfants des pays sous-développés ne survivent les périls de la première année que pour aborder une période tout aussi dangereuse.

En bref, saleté et malnutrition sont les grands coupables.

Je ne vais pas succomber à la tentation de vous citer, page après page, tout ce qu'on a pu découvrir sur la situation lamentable des enfants qui, de nos jours, vivent un peu partout sur notre globe. Mais je veux en souligner la conclusion pertinente, c'est à dire que les conditions de vie de la population tout entière des pays sous-développés doivent changer si l'on veut que la vie des enfants change. Et me voilà revenue à mes premières constatations : la production agricole doit être réorganisée, la production industrielle augmentée et l'économie en général améliorée.

Sinon, où pourrions-nous, finalement, trouver les quantités de nourriture suffisantes? Aujourd'hui, les pays qui ont le plus d'enfants importent les produits alimentaires que nous, pays riches, avons en surplus. Une partie de ces importations est payée – c'est le cas, je crois, de presque tout le blé canadien exporté – et une autre partie est distribuée gratuitement, dans le cadre de certains programmes d'assistance, comme le plan US PL 480. La communauté internationale se trouve confrontée par la nécessité d'établir un programme d'alimentation mondiale très important et d'une durée d'au moins vingt ans. Mais sûrement de telles importations ne peuvent devenir permanentes, à moins, bien entendu, que ces pays ne se mettent à produire, dans la même proportion, des marchandises dont nos pays ont absolument besoin, ce qui leur donnerait alors un véritable pouvoir d'achat.

Et le paradoxe persiste, le paradoxe entre pauvreté et richesse. Ce déséquilibre entre besoins et ressources, voilà le dilemme avec lequel les enfants du monde sont aux prises. Leur souffrance à cause de ce paradoxe est une des caractéristiques les plus inhumaines, les plus intolérables, les plus impardonnables de notre époque.

Tout cela aboutit au credo que doivent adopter les travailleurs sociaux et tous ceux qui se penchent sur les problèmes sociaux : il n'existe pas de raccourci permettant d'aider les enfants, si nous ne pouvons amener le pays tout entier où vivent ces enfants à atteindre ce que nous considérons, au 20ième siècle, un niveau de vie décent.

Il y a toutefois certains carrefours, certaines perspectives, où le sort des enfants peut passer au premier plan. Il y a à mon avis deux secteurs, et peut être pas plus de deux, où un effort acharné, déterminé, de la part de tous ceux qui se consacrent à l'enfance est indispensable. Je veux les isoler pour que nous leur accordions davantage d'attention et pour vous demander d'y penser et, si possible, dans l'avenir, de faire quelque chose de nouveau et de constructif à ce sujet. L'un est l'énigme de l'explosion de la population, l'autre, le défi fantastique posé par l'accélération du progrès par l'entremise de l'éducation.

Bien entendu, je n'ai pas l'intention de vous soumettre une thèse sur le problème socio-économique de l'accroissement de la population. Nous connaissons tous les chiffres en cause, et nous savons que la population du monde a dépassé en 1960 les trois milliards et aura probablement plus que doublé à la fin du siècle, malgré le spectre de la famine qui se dresse partout. C'est une véritable catastrophe mondiale. C'est au tour des pays ayant une population nombreuse de connaître les effets du déséquilibre entre taux de natalité et taux de mortalité que les pays d'Europe, avec une population moins nombreuse, ont connu il y a un siècle environ. A ce moment-là sont apparues les « décades de pauvreté », aujourd'hui oubliées, mais qui, entre autres, ont causé l'émigration en masse. Aujourd'hui je voudrais replacer cette énigme dans le contexte plus intime de la famille.

Cela a déjà été fait de façon impressionnante au Congrès de la population mondial à Rome, en 1954, lorsque le Pape a déclaré que c'était la responsabilité de chaque famille de n'avoir pas plus d'enfants qu'elle ne peut en prendre soin. Il y a longtemps que je me préoccupe du problème de la population et, à mon avis, c'est bien l'attitude à prendre lorsqu'il s'agit des régions misérables du globe. C'est le destin de la famille qu'il faut considérer avant tout, sa santé, la santé de la mère et des enfants qui sont déjà là et leurs chances d'avoir une alimentation convenable, les soins et le bien-être voulus, et non des principes abstraits sur le nombre d'enfants que doit comporter une famille et le taux d'augmentation des populations. Si c'est l'attitude que nous adoptons, il en découle qu'il est indispensable de renseigner la famille sur les méthodes de contrôle des naissances, en insistant sur l'espacement des maternités plus que sur leur suppression. Ces renseignements devraient être mis à la disposition des familles dès la première grossesse. On devrait charger de ce soin les maternités et centres de puériculture qui s'occupent de la famille avant et après la naissance, les sages-femmes et les médecins en général. De cette façon on forgerait une chaîne solide pour sauvegarder le principe sur lequel les nations membres sont tombées d'accord lors de la dernière réunion de l'OMS, à savoir que « chaque famille a le droit de décider du nombre d'enfants qu'elle veut ». Il s'est produit un remarquable changement dans les opinions officielles de certains organismes de l'ONU, au cours de ces deux dernières années, et l'OMS, la Commission chargée de la population et la FAO se sont prononcées en faveur d'un appui pratique donné au contrôle des naissances. L'UNICEF lui-même, à sa dernière réunion du conseil d'administration, a, sans toutefois se prononcer de façon formelle, décidé de façon nettement positive de mettre la question à l'ordre du jour de sa prochaine réunion. Le monde bouge, et il bouge de telle façon que notre situation à nous, pays évolués, devient quelque peu ironique : les habitants des pays pauvres veulent le contrôle des naissances, il existe maint travaux le prouvant, et leurs dirigeants l'ont inclus dans leurs plans et dans leur budgets. Tandis que, chez nous, il faut lutter de façon individuelle contre l'inertie publique.

Il est indispensable d'enrayer l'explosion de la population, pour sauvegarder les enfants. Voilà un des sujets sur lesquels je me sens obligée d'insister, en même temps que sur ceux de côtés économiques. La seconde cause que je veux plaider, c'est celle de l'emploi mieux dirigé de l'éducation comme moyen d'améliorer le sort des continents sous-développés et surtout le sort des enfants à la génération suivante.

Je n'ai pas l'intention de vous ennuyer avec des statistiques, et je sais que je n'en ai pas besoin pour prouver ce que j'avance. Vous n'ignorez pas que dans les pays pauvres, le majorité de la population est illettrée, ce qui veut dire que les maisons sont des foyers d'ignorance amorphe. Les gens n'ont aucune fenêtre ouverte sur le monde. Evidemment, je simplifie le problème. Les chiffres varient de 4 pourcent d'individus ayant quelque instruction dans des pays comme le Népal et l'Afghanistan jusqu'à 66 pourcent dans certains autres pays sous-développés. Peut-être est-ce peindre le tableau en couleurs trop sombres ? Nous pourrions nous dire que le nombre des enfants inscrits dans des écoles a énormément augmenté. Une des principales ambitions de ces pays, dès qu'ils ont obtenu leur indépendance, c'est de fournir des écoles à leurs enfants. L'UNESCO nous rappelle, au moyen de statistiques, que « l'on a pu organiser 90 millions de scolarités supplémentaires » dans une courte période de 7 ans, dans les années '50. Mais – et c'est diabolique ! – à cause de l'augmentation simultanée du nombre d'enfants, la proportion d'enfants à l'école a augmenté de façon bien moins sensible. En se servant des mêmes points de comparaison, on arrive seulement à de 10.2 à 12 pourcent de toute la population. C'est ainsi que la proportion de ceux qui sont privés de la chance de s'instruire reste dangereusement statique.

Je me demande si nous comprenons bien ce que signifie l'état de friche de ces esprits d'enfants. Cela veut dire qu'il y a une majorité d'enfants qui grandissent sans profiter du fait qu'ils vivent au 20ième siècle. Pour eux, les conditions de vie demeurent celles du Moyen-Age. Nous perdons chaque jour des jeunes qui pourraient connaître une vie très différente. Nous perdons chaque année une génération qui n'est pas préparée à l'avenir d'une manière qui soit synonyme de progrès. Ayant visité ou travaillé dans les trois continents sous-développés, j'ose ajouter que même les jeunes qui arrivent à se frayer un chemin à l'école sont bien souvent aux prises avec un système pédagogique désuet et indigeste qui ne leur ouvre aucune fenêtre sur le monde et ne leur forge pas les outils nécessaires pour tracer des chemins nouveaux, des écoles qui, surtout parce qu'elles héritent de la tradition occidentale, leur donnent une éducation maladaptée, de type colonial, au lieu de les préparer à une économie dynamique et à la liberté politique.

J'ai éprouvé le besoin de vous présenter ce qui, à mon avis, constitue les deux impératifs catégoriques si nous voulons que les enfants de ces pays connaissent un certain bien-être : l'explosion de la population qui les attend, et la renaissance éducative qui leur est due. En comparaison, les programmes spécialisés de bien-être sur le logement, l'adoption, les allocations familiales, oui, même le complément de l'alimentation et l'anéantissement des maladies endémiques, perdent de leur importance. Il faut avant tout que la population soit juste assez nombreuse pour qu'on puisse faire face à ses problèmes sur le plan social et lui ouvrir les avenues du savoir. Et l'éducation des adultes compte autant, sinon plus, que celle des enfants, si l'on veut permettre à ses populations de se mettre au travail et d'améliorer leur propre sort. Et il ne faut pas négliger le fait qu'en instaurant une éducation moderne, de nouvelles attitudes à l'égard de la santé, de l'hygiène, du contrôle des naissances, peuvent arriver à créer une réaction en chaîne et à faire se multiplier et se propager chaque étape vers le progrès. Je suis convaincue que, vu sous l'angle de l'histoire mondiale, les pays riches ne peuvent mieux faire que d'offrir leur appui, sur une grande échelle, à un programme mondial d'aide à l'éducation, avec matériel scolaire, livres, bibliothèques, laboratoires, toutes ces conditions onéreuses de la marche accélérée vers le progrès.

Voilà tout ce qu'il m'est possible de faire pour remplir mon rôle et vous inciter à réfléchir sur la situation lamentable de la grande majorité des enfants dans le monde.

Mais que se passe-t-il plus près de nous ? J'ai suggéré tout à l'heure que tout n'était pas pour le mieux dans le meilleur des mondes occidentaux. Toutefois, en comparant point par point les besoins que nous venons de passer en revue dans les pays sous-développés, et en comparant avec ce qui se passe chez nous, il faut bien admettre que les besoins élémentaires sont satisfaits, et les tâches élémentaires remplies, dans les pays plus évolués.

Bien entendu on peut toujours trouver des lacunes dans notre législation sociale, réclamer davantage encore d'instruction, surtout à l'âge pré-scolaire, insister sur toutes les formes d'humanisation des soins aux handicapés physiques, mentaux et sociaux. On pourrait établir une liste de désiderata dans nos pays, mais ils vous sont tellement familiers déjà qu'il est inutile de vous les énumérer au cours de cette brève étude des problèmes mondiaux. De plus la liste et la place sur la liste de ces divers perfectionnements et adaptations varient selon les pays. Nous n'avons toutefois pas besoin de chercher loin pour nous apercevoir qu'un des problèmes sociaux les plus en vue et les plus angoissants est commun à toutes les nations. On le nomme d'une manière générale « le problème de la jeunesse », ce qui est un euphémisme.

Partout nous sommes étonnés de la nouveauté et de l'acuité des problèmes auxquels on donne des noms différents selon l'angle sous lequel on l'envisage : délinquence juvénile, alcoolisme et narcomanie, indiscipline chez les étudiants, effervescence intellectuelle, négligence et excentricité vestimentaires, amour du bruit qui n'est pas sans avoir une nuance d'agressivité, ou encore le manque d'expression et l'apathie des jeunes qui errent dans nos rues. Je ne veux pas me mettre à analyser le phénomène du malaise social chez les jeunes, encore moins me mettre à prêcher. Il suffit de dire que dans nos sociétés évoluées, nous ne sommes pas arrivés à créer une transition « en souplesse » de l'enfance à l'âge adulte. Nous n'avons pas réussi à trouver une structure permettant aux jeunes de passer harmonieusement de la dépendance à l'indépendance, selon leur propre rythme de croissance.

Nous ne revenons pas avec nostalgie sur l'époque où les enfants étaient envoyés au travail avant même d'en avoir la force, mais j'estime que le système de coordonnées qui nous ont servi à diviser la vie en « âges » est encore dicté par la situation qui existait il y a plusieurs générations, quand pour la majorité des enfants le départ de l'école signifiait l'entrée dans le monde du travail – une magnifique harmonisation de règles sociales que nous avons tous aidé à codifier en nous basant sur les recommandations de ILO. Ce que notre imagination n'a encore pu concevoir, c'est l'effet de ce que j'appellerai l'explosion de l'éducation. Je crois qu'au Canada 60 pourcent des moins de 20 ans sont en ce moment à l'école et, en Suède, nous nous attendons à ce que ce soit, d'ici dix ans, le cas de 70 à 80 pourcent de jeunes de 16 à 20 ans. Le cycle de la vie change quand un nombre prédominant de notre population s'apprête à consacrer à sa formation les deux premières décades de sa vie. En termes simplifiés, cela signifie que l'âge légal du mariage et du vote se situe maintenant à l'intérieur de la période d'éducation. Le processus de préparation à la maturité dans ces domaines très importants – la fondation d'un foyer, la participation aux affaires civiques – va maintenant de pair avec la soumission à la discipline académique et avec la dépendance économique.

Cette évolution vers une période non-productive considérablement prolongée, qui va jusqu'à la maturité biologique et sexuelle et ne s'accompagne d'aucun changement dans nos cadres et institutions, ne manquera pas de surprendre les historiens de l'avenir. Nous qui vivons en pleine période de changement social avons à peine commencé de reconnaître le défi qui nous est jeté. Nous lamenter sur la moralité des jeunes n'est sûrement pas le moyen de le relever.

Ce qu'une réorganisation constructive de nos formes sociales et de nos modes de vie personnels exige à présent, je suis incapable de vous le dire. Il faudrait peut-être consacrer tout un congrès à ce seul problème. On a commencé ici et là d'adapter les conditions socio-économiques. Grâce à l'abolition des frais de scolarité, aux nombreuses bourses, etc., les états très engagés dans les systèmes de bien-être public sont arrivés à couvrir partiellement les frais qu'il faut encourir parce qu'on est jeune. Mais est-ce suffisant pour garantir l'indépendance ? Et même, dans la majorité des cas, cela permet-il d'établir des budgets complets que les jeunes administrent eux-mêmes ? Grâce à des arrangements pratiques, appartements familiaux, maternelles, sur les campus, on a augmenté la possibilité de se marier pour les étudiants. J'ose pourtant douter qu'il s'agisse là d'un système durable. Quand on voit, par exemple qu'à l'Université d'Uppsala, un tiers des étudiants sont mariés, on ne peut s'empêcher de se demander s'il ne s'agit pas là pour beaucoup de mariages précipités pour acquérir, de la seule façon socialement acceptable, une certaine liberté, un certain statut adulte. Là encore, je précise, je ne critique pas. J'essaye seulement de démêler ce qui se cache, sur le plan social, derrière ce nouveau et fantastique défi, et les compromis auxquels on arrive pour tenter d'y faire face.

Ce qu'il faut avant tout, c'est un changement radical d'optique. Le concept même du cycle de vie humaine ne correspond plus à ce qu'il était. L'adolescence se fond avec l'âge adulte dans des conditions nouvelles. Et la vieillesse est évidemment repoussée, la longévité prolongée et l'apparence et le comportement des gens âgés rajeunissent. Au cours de ces deux périodes cruciales, il nous faut des mesures plus imaginatives qu'une scolarité prolongée pour les jeunes et une retraite pour les vieux. A ces deux groupes il faut une participation plus active à la vie, et plus d'indépendance. Dans les deux cas, j'estime personnellement qu'il faudrait avant tout surmonter le conflit entre les années productrices et les autres, qu'elles soient pré- ou post-productrices. Elles sont maintenant devenues trop longues et trop dénuées de sens. Pour les jeunes, il nous faut trouver des modes de transition appropriés. Peut-être faudrait-il instituer des écoles ou des camps, où le travail productif et rémunéré irait de pair avec les études. Ce n'est que par de tels moyens que nous arriverons à l'autre but : l'abandon graduel par les parents de leur autorité et de leur surveillance, un abandon des rênes qu'il est si raisonnable de réclamer, mais, en fait, si difficile à réaliser.

Enfin je veux laisser à ce congrès le soin de résoudre le problème de savoir lequel de ces types de difficultés le monde devrait pouvoir résoudre en premier. Trouverons-nous un moyen de sauvegarder les besoins élémentaires de millions d'enfants dans les pays qui sont trop pauvres pour eux, ou donnerons-nous aux jeunes de pays qui leur ont donné tout – ou presque tout – le reste, une participation plus respectée, indépendante et active dans une vie qui aura, par conséquent, plus de sens pour eux?

Roads to Maturity: The Basic Issues

DR. ALAN ROSS

THIS CONFERENCE is forever in Dr. Myrdal's debt for that magnificent discussion last evening of the challenging world situation. As we listened, it was not hard to recognize that we as individuals all have a place—a role to play. She has given us the broad view. Yet broad landscapes are made up of small landscapes, difficult perhaps to see at a distance but still playing an essential part in the total picture. The part I must now play is to lead you down from the mountain to the market-place and to introduce you to a discussion of the pressing problems of the day in Canada. I expect you will find yourselves looking back over your shoulders as you come down and this is as it should be. I am sure that much of Dr. Myrdal's address will keep coming back to us all long after this Conference has ended. In the same way, much of what will be said as we meet together will continue to stir and stimulate us in the months ahead.

To introduce these three days of discussion, I would like to deal quite briefly with a few of the many crucial issues that have kept cropping up in the reports from local committees. I think we simply must face these issues squarely if this Conference is going to justify its existence.

First of all, we must recognize the call for wider communication and effective co-operation between all professions that serve this country. This is to be expected, for it was from this need that this Conference really sprang. In the five years since our first meeting, strange as it may seem, this need for co-operation has increased; it always seems to be that, as co-operation increases, opportunities for more co-operation keep opening up.

For instance, a generation ago, a child with cerebral palsy was taken to his doctor who found himself with hands tied by lack of any real knowledge of the disease, lack of community interest, lack of professional interest, and lack of educational opportunities for his patient. He might or might not have some insight into the implications that the situation had for the child's parents, for his friends, for the whole family structure, for the school, and for the community. He was apt to have little comfort and no real programme to offer these parents. Now, this is recognized as a situation that can only be adequately served by a team. Now, such a child is brought before a group which includes, aside from experts in medical care, such people as teachers, psychologists, social service workers, and occupational and speech therapists. Lines of communication are set up, individual discussions begin, and opportunities for co-operative effort are opened wide.

One of our tasks in the three days of the conference must surely be to study ways and means whereby this principle, this team approach, can be extended and applied to other problems in health, in education, in welfare. I use cerebral palsy as an example of co-operation between disciplines within the health sciences field. It is relatively easy in this field for us to work together. If Dr. McCreary has his way at the University of British Columbia, and I am sure that he will, not only will the medical sciences and those sometimes called "paramedical," all work together but they will also be trained together and will, therefore, be in a better position to develop co-operative programmes when the opportunity arises.

Since it is easy, and at the moment perhaps especially pertinent, to find examples of weakness in government, let me use this vulnerable institution to illustrate the need for inter-departmental communication. A camp for diabetic children recently applied to the government for support on the basis that such a camp was dealing with sick children, teaching them and their parents to live with the disease, rehabilitating them to society, preventing physical and emotional complications, and fitting them for the normal functions of childhood, adolescence, and adult life. The camp authorities are still being referred from one ministry to another. From Health to Welfare, to Youth, to Education, and back to Health. In some provinces, notably the one in which we meet, this difficulty has been appreciated and co-ordinating facilities are being set up to link department with department and ministry with ministry. But isolation is not confined to government. We find it, if we look for it, in universities, in hospitals, in schools—in fact, in institutions of all kinds.

It is apparent that the care of children and youth is even more directly inhibited by distressingly little person-to-person discussion across the transparent but solid partitions between disciplines. Doctors so seldom sit down with teachers, social service workers with employers, nurses with occupational therapists, educators with experts in rehabilitation, juvenile court judges with doctors, to discuss the needs of a particular child. It is not enough for us to talk, as we must in a conference of this kind, about the child in the abstract. This Conference and its on-going committees must devise ways and means whereby the problems of individual children can be met. It is time-consuming but it must be done. Last evening one of our guests asked me if this group of people were theoreticians and I was glad to be able to assure him that while in a sense we were, we were also accustomed to dealing with individual children.

Even more basic to this need is the need to foster direct communication with the child himself which, as all of us know, is through channels that are as much unconscious as conscious. How little interest, time, and skill we are ready to devote to the art of listening to what children have to tell us—even less to feeling the unspoken vibrations that are in the air of every home we visit. Fundamentally this sort of communication requires not only tolerance and understanding but sensitivity and warmth and the power to radiate all these to others. To some, this comes naturally; for others, it must be learned. Nowhere is the need for the communication between individuals more apparent than in dealing with that great institution of learning by the trial and error method, the family. Our deliberations and discussion will of course keep reverting to the family. It is an interesting fact that the family exerts immeasurably important influences upon society yet blows with the wind, reflecting the kaleidoscopic changes going on in the world in which it functions. It is a bulwark of society in almost every culture, yet is amazingly adaptable to change. In physiology there is a dictum that function determines form. In our considerations this week, let us not forget the functions, in many respects the new functions, that the family is being called upon to serve. It is little wonder that its form is changing. It is little wonder that our forebears would hardly recognize the modern family as the same institution they had known. One of our prime tasks at this Conference must be to look at family structure, appreciate that its architecture is modern and functional, and be prepared to discard some of the gingerbread that adorned it in the past. But, let us first make quite sure that what looks like gingerbread is, in reality, superfluous. Certainly we must find ways of strengthening the foundations on which the family is built. But let us accept, even expect, changes in this institution as in everywhere else in society.

Any group of people sitting down to discuss the roads to maturity and the development of responsible Canadians must come to grips with the woefully inadequate environment that faces the child "born into disadvantage," to borrow a colourful term. I am thinking, of course, of the Eskimo, the Indian, the Doukhobors, and, to a lesser extent, other minority ethnic groups. How little time, real concern, and financing has gone into any intelligent inquiry into the plight of these fellow countrymen of ours—into the future that this country of ours is offering them—into the roadblocks that they meet at every turn.

I am thinking, too, of the children who are growing up in the multi-problem families of our industrial communities and our complete failure to find any long-term sound approach to this problem that dates back far into social history. Let me illustrate, for those who are not faced with this breeding ground of anti-social behaviour that threatens to undermine the life of our great cities. A so-called "battered baby" was brought to our clinic a few weeks ago because of a long-standing limp. She was found to have the all-too-common multiple fractures characteristic of this disability. Inquiry revealed a family of seven children under eight years of age, their mother unmarried and six months pregnant, their "father" chronically unemployed, their home in a deplorable state. This mother, it turned out, came from exactly the same kind of home on the next street. It was decided to place two of these children in a small convalescent home for toddlers and to set up an intensive programme of rehabilitation for the family. The social welfare court was asked for legal advice and help. After thoughtful consideration the judgment has just come down that these children are to be removed from the home. Now this is a difficult, expensive, and time-consuming task. It is radical surgery that goes contrary to accepted welfare precepts. But in the health field radical surgery in carefully selected cases has resulted in some unbelievable cures. Can our society afford such measures? Can our society afford not to take such measures, when they are indicated? Do they encroach on human rights? Do they threaten the dignity of the child or his value in society? I would submit that this week this Conference has an opportunity to consider such questions, to study in depth the disadvantaged child and his environment, and to set in motion discussions that may take an entirely new and objective look at problems such as these that have so far baffled us all. Perhaps we can devise some entirely new approaches to old problems.

But it is not always new approaches that we need. So often we know what should be done and yet, in our democratic society, we lack the organization, the personnel, and perhaps even the will to bring essential services within the grasp of those who need them most. Why do we, in the midst of such tremendous prosperity, find ourselves so lacking in services such as nursery facilities, foster homes, homemakers, family planning, pre-natal and well-baby clinics, to say nothing of progressive health programmes in the schools? Why have we such difficulty and why must it take so long to bring to Canadian children and Canadian homes the good things that are available and that we know foster responsible citizenship?

In many areas our greatest opportunities lie, I think, in devising preventive programmes. The prevention of disease is accepted as the ultimate goal of medicine. Every medical school has a department where teaching and research related to preventive medicine, epidemiology, and public health are being actively pursued. Great strides have been taken and a host of diseases have, or can now be, completely eliminated. But I would submit that less emphasis is being put on this approach in education and welfare. We have been concerned about, and tried to help, the child with a normal intelligence who is having difficulty in learning. It is only in very recent years that we have come around to asking ourselves "why." We have only just begun research projects to determine how these old but pressing difficulties come about and how they might be prevented. In the welfare field the roadblocks are numerous and complicated. Even though important moves have been made by thoughtful and diligent workers, the road has been strewn with obstacles. The daily load of communities, families, and individuals that need rehabilitation distracts us from basic studies of causes and their remedy. It is not enough to remove roadblocks. They keep reappearing like mushrooms and unless their source can be found and eradicated our efforts must be classed as ineffective and misdirected.

Let us then look for causes as we consider the problems that beset developing Canadians. Let us remind those who say that the poor are always with us that it was only a century ago in England that the appearance of cholera each summer was considered as inevitable as the return of swallows in Spring.

At the risk of boredom, let me remind you again not only of the rapid changes that are going on in society but of the accelerating speed with which these changes are coming. It is not enough to meet the problems of today. Tomorrow will be upon us before we know it and our considerations must keep the future always before us. Three relative newcomers are on our doorstep: medicare, automation, and population control. Each is revolutionary; each brings its threats and its promises. Each, too, will have its effect on all our lives and particularly on the lives of the children with whom we work.

I have touched on only a few of the issues that seem to me of paramount importance and which have been brought before this Conference: communication, co-ordination, the changing position of the family in our society, children born into disadvantage, and the need for more interest in prevention. I have reminded you that medicare, automation, and population control are vital problems of the day. Many others will crowd in on us. Few of them can be solved here in three short days. But ideas can be born. Plans for fact-finding on critical issues can be set in motion. Our present knowledge can be critically examined and it is to be hoped that in some instances a framework for action can be constructed. These I think are some of the challenges as we sit down together this morning.

Vers la maturité: les grands problèmes

Le congrès a une véritable dette de reconnaissance à l'égard du Dr Myrdal pour la façon magistrale dont elle a décrit la situation dans le monde. En l'écoutant, il devenait facile de comprendre qu'en tant qu'individus nous y avons tous notre rôle à jouer. Elle nous a brossé un tableau d'ensemble. Mais les tableaux d'ensemble sont faits de petits tableaux qu'il est peut être difficile de voir de loin, mais qui sont partie intégrante du tout. Mon rôle est de vous guider du sommet de la montagne à la place du marché, et de vous inviter à trois journées de discussions sur les problèmes canadiens pressants. Je m'attends à vous voir jeter un coup d'œil en arrière pendant la descente, et c'est très bien ainsi. Je suis certain que nous nous remémorerons les paroles du Dr Myrdal longtemps après la fin du congrès, tout comme une grande partie de ce qui se dira au cours de ce congrès continuera de nous stimuler et de nous faire réfléchir au cours des mois qui vont suivre.

En introduction à ces trois jours de discussion, je voudrais passer brièvement en revue quelques-uns des problèmes les plus sérieux que font ressortir les rapports des comités provinciaux. Je pense que nous devrons, simplement, faire face à ces problèmes, si la conférence doit justifier son existence.

D'abord, il nous faut admettre le besoin d'une communication plus intense, d'une collaboration plus efficace, entre toutes les professions qui servent les intérêts du pays. Cela, il fallait s'y attendre, puisque c'est, en réalité, de ce besoin qu'est née la Conférence canadienne de l'enfance. Au cours des cinq années qui se sont écoulées depuis notre première réunion, si étrange que cela puisse paraître, ce besoin de coopération a augmenté. Car il semble bien qu'au fur et à mesure que la coopération progresse, il naît de nouvelles raisons de coopérer. Par exemple, il y a quelques années, on amenait l'enfant atteint de paralysie cérébrale au médecin qui se trouvait lié par le manque de connaissances précises sur la maladie, le manque d'intérêt de la société, le manque d'intérêt professionnel et le manque de possibilités d'instruction du patient. Il pouvait se faire une idée plus ou moins claire de ce que la situation représentait pour les parents de l'enfant, pour les amis, pour toute la cellule familiale, pour l'école et pour la communauté. En général, le médecin ne pouvait guère réconforter la famille ni lui offrir un programme réel. Maintenant, on s'est rendu compte que ce type de situation exigeait les services d'une équipe. L'enfant est examiné par un groupe qui comprend, outre l'équipe médicale, des instituteurs, des psychologues, des travailleurs sociaux, des spécialistes en ergothérapie et en orthophonie. On établit des contacts, des discussions sur le plan individuel ont lieu, et on crée toutes les occasions pour un effort commun.

Parmi les tâches qui nous incombent, au cours de ces trois jours, figurera bien certainement celle de savoir dans quelle mesure on peut généraliser ce travail d'équipe et s'en servir pour d'autres problèmes de santé, d'éducation et de bien-être. Je me suis servi de la paralysie cérébrale comme exemple, car il nous est relativement facile de collaborer activement entre professions dans ce domaine. Si le Dr McCreary peut faire ce qu'il veut à l'University of British Columbia, et je suis sûr qu'il y arrivera, non seulement les diverses branches de la médecine mais aussi les disciplines qu'on appelle parfois « para-médicales », s'associeront plus étroitement.

Comme il est facile – et peut-être, en ce moment, pertinent – de découvrir des fautes et des erreurs dans un gouvernement, je vais me servir de cette vulnérable institution pour illustrer le besoin de rapports entre divers services. Un camp pour enfants diabétiques a, il y a quelque temps, fait une demande de subvention auprès du gouvernement en expliquant que ce camp était destiné à des enfants malades, qu'il leur apprenait, à eux et à leurs parents, comment vivre avec leur maladie, les réadaptait à la vie sociale, prévenait ou tentait de prévenir les complications d'ordre physique ou affectif, et les rendait aptes à vivre en enfants, adolescents et plus tard, en adultes normaux. Les directeurs de ce camp continuent de se faire renvoyer d'un ministère à un autre : de la Santé au Bien-Etre, à la Jeunesse, à l'Education et de nouveau à la Santé. Dans certaines provinces, et en particulier dans celle où nous nous réunissons, on a pris conscience de ces difficultés et on s'est arrangé pour créer des liens entre services et entre ministères. Mais ce splendide isolement ne se trouve pas seulement au gouvernement. Si nous cherchons bien, nous en trouverons des exemples dans les universités, les hôpitaux, les écoles, en fait, dans toutes les institutions.

Il est visible que les soins à l'enfance et à la jeunesse sont encore plus directement compromis par les petites discussions individuelles qui ont lieu et les cloisons transparentes mais solides qui se dressent entre disciplines. Les médecins siègent rarement avec les professeurs, les travailleurs sociaux avec les employeurs, les infirmières avec les ergothérapeutes, les éducateurs avec les spécialistes de la rééducation, les juges des tribunaux de l'enfance avec les médecins, pour discuter des besoins d'un enfant en particulier. Car il ne suffit pas de parler de l'enfance sur le plan abstrait, comme nous le faisons dans un congrès de ce genre, il faut que nous – et les comités qui suivront cette conférence – trouvions les moyens de résoudre les problèmes des enfants sur le plan individuel et concret. Cela prend du temps, mais c'est indispensable. Hier soir, un de nos invités m'a demandé si ce groupe se composait de théoriciens. J'ai été heureux de pouvoir lui répondre que si, dans une certaine mesure, c'est ce que nous sommes tous, nous sommes tous également habitués à nous occuper directement d'enfants.

Plus essentielle encore que ce besoin est la nécessité de créer des rapports directs avec l'enfant lui-même et cela, nous le savons, par des voies qui sont souvent aussi inconscientes que conscientes. Combien peu d'intérêt, de temps et de talent sommes-nous prêts à consacrer à l'art d'écouter ce que nous disent les enfants, et encore moins à l'art de percevoir les ondes qui émanent de tous les foyers que nous visitons. Fondamentalement, cela demande non seulement compréhension et tolérance, mais aussi sensibilité et chaleur humaine, et la capacité de faire rayonner ces qualités. Pour certains, c'est tout naturel. D'autres devront l'apprendre. Et nulle part le besoin de communications individuelles ne se fait-il autant sentir que dans cette institution où l'on apprend au hasard des erreurs et des maladresses, la famille. Car nos délibérations, nos discussions, en reviennent bien entendu toujours à la famille. Il vaut la peine de noter que la famille exerce sur la société une influence énorme, mais qu'en même temps elle reflète les changements kaléidoscopiques qui ont lieu dans le monde. C'est un des fondements de presque toutes les cultures, mais elle est prodigieusement adaptable. En physiologie, on dit que la fonction détermine la structure. Dans nos recherches de cette semaine, n'oublions pas les fonctions, dans bien des cas de nouvelles fonctions, que doit remplir la famille. Il n'est pas étonnant que les structures changent. Il n'est pas étonnant de penser que nos ancêtres ne reconnaitraient peut-être pas l'institution de la famille.

Une de nos tâches principales, à ce congrès, c'est d'étudier la cellule familiale, d'évaluer si sa structure est moderne et fonctionnelle, se préparer à rejeter tout le rococo qui l'ornait il y a des années. Mais assurons-nous d'abord que ce rococo est bien superflu. Nous devons trouver des moyens de raffermir les fondations sur lesquelles est construite la famille. Mais il faut accepter, et même s'attendre à des changements dans ce domaine comme partout ailleurs.

Un groupe d'individus qui se réunit pour discuter des voies de la maturité et de la formation d'une génération de Canadiens conscients de leurs responsabilités doit prendre en considération le milieu lamentable dans lequel grandit l'enfant qui naît dans les groupes sociaux défavorisés : je pense évidemment aux Esquimaux, aux Indiens, aux doukhobors, et, dans un degré moindre, à tous les membres des minorités ethniques. Combien peu de temps, d'intérêt et d'argent on a consacré à l'étude du sort pitoyable de ces compatriotes, à l'avenir qui s'offre à eux et aux obstacles contre lesquels ils buttent sans cesse.

Je pense également aux enfants qui naissent dans les familles à problèmes multiples, dans nos grandes villes, et à notre échec total pour trouver une solution durable et satisfaisante à ce problème qui remonte loin dans notre histoire sociale. Permettez-moi d'en donner un exemple pour ceux qui ne seraient pas familiers avec ce terrain où germent toutes les conduites anti-sociales qui risquent de saper la vie des grandes villes. Un « bébé maltraité » nous a été amené il y a quelques temps, souffrant d'une boîterie persistante. On s'est aperçu qu'elle avait subi les multiples fractures qui sont hélas caractéristiques de ce type d'infirmité. A l'enquête, on a trouvé une famille de sept enfants de moins de huit ans, mère célibataire enceinte de six mois, père en chômage chronique, maison dans un état déplorable. On a également appris que la mère venait d'une famille semblable, dans la rue voisine. On a décidé de placer deux des enfants dans une maison de convalescence pour tout petits et d'organiser un programme intensif de réadaptation pour la famille, en demandant les conseils et l'appui de la cour juvénile. Après mûre réflexion, le jugement de la cour vient d'être passé : il faut retirer les enfants aux parents. Voilà une tâche difficile. C'est une opération radicale, et contraire à tous les principes du bien-être. Mais, en médecine, une opération radicale judicieusement prescrite peut avoir des résultats étonnants. Notre société peut-elle se permettre de prendre de telles mesures ? Peut-elle se permettre de ne pas les prendre quand elles sont nécessaires ? Est-ce un empiètement sur les droits de l'individu, une atteinte à la dignité de l'enfant et à sa valeur sociale ? A mon avis, cette semaine, le Congrès a la chance de pouvoir considérer ces questions, d'étudier sérieusement l'enfance malheureuse et son milieu, et d'amorcer des discussions qui pourraient envisager de façon radicalement nouvelle des problèmes comme ceux-ci, qui nous ont si souvent rendus perplexes. Peut-être pourrons-nous trouver des solutions neuves à de vieux problèmes.

Mais ce ne sont pas toujours de solutions nouvelles que nous avons besoin. Dans bien des cas, nous savons ce qu'il faut faire et pourtant, dans notre société démocratique, nous n'avons pas l'organisation, le personnel, peut-être même pas le désir, de procurer les services essentiels à ceux qui en ont tant besoin. Pourquoi, au milieu de notre prospérité fabuleuse, avons-nous si peu de maternités, de crèches, d'aides familiales, de foyers adoptifs, de centres de régulation des naissances, de pouponnières, sans parler de programmes sanitaires dans les écoles ? Pourquoi avons-nous tant de mal à apporter aux enfants et aux foyers canadiens tous les bienfaits qui formeraient des citoyens solides ?

Dans bien des domaines il faudrait nous occuper de prévention. En médecine, on estime que c'est là le but final. Toutes les écoles de médecine ont un service où l'on s'occupe activement d'enseignement et de recherches dans les domaines de la médecine préventive, de l'épidémiologie et de l'hygiène publique. On a beaucoup progressé et nombre de maladies ont disparu. Mais je suis certain que dans les domaines de l'éducation et du bien-être, il n'en est pas ainsi. Nous nous sommes souciés d'étudier l'enfant d'intelligence normale avec difficultés scolaires, et de l'aider. Mais ce n'est que récemment que nous nous sommes vraiment penchés sur le « pourquoi » du problème. Nous venons seulement de mettre en train des programmes de recherches pour déterminer les causes de ce vieux problème si important, et ce qu'on peut faire pour le prévenir. Dans le domaine du bien-être, les obstacles sont nombreux et compliqués. Même si des travailleurs dévoués et consciencieux ont permis de gros progrès, la route est jalonnée de déceptions. La tâche quotidienne de réparer, de rapiécer, que ce soit à l'échelon communautaire, familial ou individuel, nous empêche de nous consacrer à l'étude des causes et aux remèdes. Ce n'est pas assez de repousser les obstacles, ils reviennent, à moins qu'on n'en détruise la source, et nos efforts seront vains.

Par conséquent, cherchons les causes, en nous occupant des problèmes qui assiègent le Canada. Et rappelons à ceux qui répètent qu'il y aura toujours des pauvres parmi nous qu'il y a à peine un siècle, en Angleterre, on estimait que le retour du choléra, tous les étés, était « aussi inévitable que le retour des hirondelles au printemps », pour citer un médecin-poète.

Au risque de vous lasser, permettez-moi de vous répéter une fois encore l'importance non seulement de l'évolution sociale, mais de la rapidité avec laquelle elle se produit. Il ne suffit pas de résoudre les problèmes d'aujourd'hui, il faut penser à demain. Trois nouveautés sont à la veille de faire leur apparition parmi nous : médicare, automation et régulation des naissances. Chacune représente une révolution, chacune est chargée de promesses et de menaces, chacune va modifier profondément nos vies et surtout celles des enfants dont nous nous occupons.

Je n'ai abordé que quelques-uns des problèmes qui me semblent avoir une importance primordiale et qui feront l'objet de vos délibérations à ce congrès : rapports et coordination, évolution de la famille dans la société, enfance malheureuse, besoin de consacrer davantage d'efforts à la prévention. Je vous ai rappelé que médicare, automation et régulation des naissances étaient des problèmes de première importance. Bien d'autres surgiront. Il ne s'agit pas de les résoudre en trois jours, mais des idées naîtront, des programmes de recherches s'organiseront. Nous pourrons évaluer de façon critique l'état actuel de nos connaissance et, je l'espère, dans certains cas commencer de passer à l'action.

Review and Commentary: I

DR. ALAN THOMAS

IN YOUR MEETINGS yesterday, you talked about the importance of listening: listening to other professionals, listening to children and youth. Perhaps anticipating this, your Conference Committee has invited me to be a listener–to listen to you. My task is to reflect on two aspects of your Conference–on the issues, the intellectual content of your discussions, and on the process in which you are all engaged–and to summarize for you each morning, the previous day's deliberations.

It occurred to me that you, as a conference, might want to know something about your own statistics. There are about 425 registrants of which 90 are from Ontario, 90 from Quebec, 32 from British Columbia, 22 from Alberta, 15 from Saskatchewan, 30 from Manitoba, 20 from New Brunswick, 20 from Nova Scotia, 4 from Prince Edward Island, and, unhappily, no one from Newfoundland. The other delegates are distinguished international guests, representatives of the federal government and the national co-operating organizations, and programme participants. The Conference affords a wide base from which to exchange skills, information, and ideas. The task is to make the most effective use of the talents, imagination, and experience here assembled.

It did not seem possible to analyze the group in terms of professional backgrounds because there are so many different and interlocking categories. Despite your obvious concern about enhancing communication among the specialists, many of the delegates are already working in more than one traditional field–across specialties. Perhaps in your discussion groups you could examine the background of the participants and from this learn how some have overcome the professional and institutional barriers in the interests of the solution of specific problems.

Conferences are for conferring. We have many in Canada, as you know, that are really rallies but this Conference has placed great emphasis on the act of conferring. A large percentage of your time will be spent in small discussion groups. It is from these that the planners expect the major achievements of this Conference, not from the platform presentations which have been designed primarily to forward the discussion in your groups.

This Conference, because it is a temporary society as all conferences are, is devoted to a specific and unique problem which, as you attest by your presence here, is not receiving adequate attention in your day-to-day affairs. While you have come together to discuss children as children you are also attempting to embody one of the most persistent of problems—the problem of inter-communication, of conveying meaning across vocabularies, professional disciplines, and institutions. In your groups you are being asked to experiment with some of the problems you are also discussing and this led yesterday to some very interesting experiences. From the kinds of things that happened I believe that there is a high degree of awareness that the struggle is with yourselves as well as with intellectual issues about which you can be detached. The nature of the discussion that took place indicated an awareness of the need to question our own activities as well as to diagnose and plan for the difficulties and problems of someone else.

In setting the keynote to the Conference, Dr. Myrdal asked us to examine four fundamental proposals. First of all, she set our deliberations in a broader scene and asked us to consider the relationship between the conditions and circumstance of our children and children in other parts of the world. Secondly, in discussing the "pre-productive" years she challenged us with the idea that we were treating some adults as children. This was an interesting contrast to our Canadian concern that we are treating some children as though they were adults. This led to a third concern, "What does being a child really mean?" One of the things Dr. Myrdal seemed to suggest was that our lexicon of relationships needs more categories than "child" and "adult." The last challenge that she raised is one that seemed to be germane to the struggles you were experiencing in your groups yesterday. She indicated two kinds of response—imagination and compassion—and said that both are legitimate and necessary ways of responding. Perhaps we need to think about our ability to be both imaginative and compassionate. Sometimes in our desire to be and to help children to become imaginative and creative, we are less preoccupied with the need that we all have to learn to be compassionate also.

This, it seems to me, was part of the process in which we were engaged yesterday. We were each making ourselves felt and each reaching out for the other. We were developing the one thing which alone makes communication possible and that is trust. While the content of our discussion was important, it was not as important as the relationships that were being established.

What was happening also, is what always seems to happen when different professions come together. There is always a certain competition over the right to define the problem—with each profession wishing to make it intelligible from his point of view. If one wins the right of definition one also wins the right to be regarded as the specialist. This is a normal and necessary undertaking—but perhaps today we will be able to move on to a deeper commitment to the solution of problems than to the maintenance of one's security through the maintenance of the status quo.

Many of your groups talked about innovation and I would suggest to you that this is a fruitful area. It is often around innovation that the professions come together since by re-defining a problem one is able to use multiple resources without conflict or damaging competition.

In addition, what was happening yesterday is part of the debate between what people say needs to be done and what existing institutions and professions say they can or will do. Because of the need to bring these two together, this kind of conference becomes necessary and valuable, for without a resolution to this conflict society would flounder—especially a society with a high investment in technical and professional competence. It is an important task that you have undertaken and one where the solutions may be difficult but unexpected.

It is also interesting to observe your willingness to challenge. There were, for example, some sharp challenges to the sacredness of the family and to our dependence upon it. There was also evident some real changes in attitude towards the family. We have been talking for decades about the transfer of responsibilities for children from the family to other institutions. What is new is the assumption by the professional establishment, or by the state, of responsibility for the family itself. The family previously was a party to society, now it has become an object of study and concern.

And there were challenges, many of them, to other institutions. We have not yet in this or any other conference to my knowledge, however, gone so far as to question what is probably one of the most imbedded and unconscious of our beliefs, belief in legislation for compulsory education. I am not suggesting that this is wrong but only that it is one of the institutional foundation stones that needs analysis and examination every bit as much as the family does.

There was one issue that you raised over and over again with some sense of despair. It is a poignant, though familiar, idea. There is not enough time! There is no time to listen to children, no time for one specialist to listen to another, no time to do the things we know we ought to do. I would suggest to you that in this context the question of "time" is completely a moral one: to decide what use is to be made of it. Maybe our despair is really a reflection of something else. We are living in a society in which we believe that there is no technical problem we cannot solve, provided we have enough money, enough time, and enough resources. We believe we will find a cure for cancer and for most diseases given the time, the research, the trained personnel, and the finances. Because of this belief, we have a tendency to turn as many problems as we can into technical ones because there our hope lies. Then we complain because we don't have the resources to do what we know we could do. It may be, however, that some of these issues are moral ones. They cannot easily be translated into technical ones and as moral problems we simply have to live with them. We have to admit, both to ourselves and to our children, that they exist. Maybe this is what Dr. Myrdal means by a need for compassion, because it requires compassion to admit a source of pain or grief which we simply do not know how to solve or remove. So on one side we are challenged again to use our imagination with respect to those problems which are technical and to apply our compassion to those that are not.

It interested me that some, not all, of your discussion of younger children tended to be on technical grounds. It tended to be about things we might do to make life more bearable, more productive for younger children, if we had the money, resources, and talents. But the discussion of teenagers involved moral questions. We do not seem quite so sure that technical achievement is going to make all that much difference for this age group. Perhaps because the older children come close to the condition of being preproductive adults, they are not so acquiescent; they are not necessarily willing to live quietly and peacefully with us. They are more willing to challenge and we find our own doubts more mirrored in them than we do in the younger. We are not quite so sure of our capacity to interpret the behaviour of teenagers in technical terms.

Because any concern about our children immediately raises a concern about ourselves, we are expressing some sense of disquiet about our responsibility for the world in which our children must grow up and some feelings of inadequacy about our capacity to help them. I think that compassion, as well as being extended to our children, needs also to be extended to ourselves for we are not totally responsible for the kind of world in which we live. After all, we are products of previous generations and when we speak, we speak not only with our own voices but with the voices of our fathers and their fathers.

I caught, in your deliberations, some sense of wanting to conceal our inadequacies from our children and youth and I think it is a matter of debate amongst you as to how much we should share with them our own difficulties. In this context, I was reminded of Silone's words when he said "The trouble with children is that they believe what adults tell them." I think this is profoundly important because we don't always hear what we tell our children; we only hear what we say as a part of our own internal struggle with ourselves. But our children don't see the struggle, they just hear the words. For this reason in talking about communication, you need to think not only of communication between yourselves but also with children. This may have been implicit in your regret that more "youth" was not present at this conference.

So, there were three major concerns included in your discussions yesterday. What can we teach our children considering the state in which we find ourselves? What do we really communicate to our children? And, finally, how much do we have to change in order to live up to our promises to our children and to do anything about the children in other parts of the world? Is it only a matter of working harder at what we are now doing or is it a matter of doing some things differently? It seems to me that the questions you were asking yesterday that laid the foundation for what you will do today, embodied the realization that each one of us must come to terms with the child within himself as well as the children and the society in which he lives.

Revue et commentaire: I

Lors de vos réunions d'hier, vous avez parlé d'écouter : d'écouter les membres des autres professions, d'écouter les enfants et les jeunes. Le comité d'organisation de ce congrès a dû prévoir vos réflexions, car il m'a invité à venir vous écouter. Ma tâche est double au cours de ce congrès : je dois refléter vos problèmes, le contenu intellectuel de vos discussions et de vos travaux, et vous résumer, chaque matin, les délibérations de la veille.

J'ai pensé qu'il vous intéresserait peut-être de prendre connaissance de quelques chiffres pertinents concernant ce congrès : il y a environ 425 inscrits, 90 de l'Ontario, 90 du Québec, 32 de la Colombie britannique, 22 d'Alberta, 15 de la Saskatchewan, 30 du Manitoba, 20 du Nouveau-Brunswick, 20 de Nouvelle-Ecosse, 4 de l'Ile du Prince Edouard. Malheureusement, personne n'est venu de Terre-Neuve. Les autres assistants sont des invités internationaux distingués, des représentants du gouvernement fédéral et des organismes associés, les conférenciers et les organisateurs. Le Congrès offre tout le champ nécessaire à un échange d'idées, de connaissances et de compétences. La tâche est d'arriver à faire le meilleur usage des talents, de l'imagination et de l'expérience qui se trouvent rassemblés ici.

Il ne semble pas possible d'analyser le groupe en termes de professions; il existe trop de catégories variées et connexes. Malgré votre souci visible d'augmenter les communications entre spécialités, un grand nombre de délégués travaillent déjà dans plus d'un secteur traditionnel et couvrent plusieurs spécialités. Peut-être, à l'intérieur de vos groupes de discussion, pourrez-vous étudier la formation professionnelle des participants et apprendre de quelque façon comment certains ont pu surmonter les barrières professionnelles et institutionnelles pour arriver à résoudre des problèmes spécifiques.

Un congrès se réunit pour délibérer. Nous en avons beaucoup au Canada qui sont simplement des rencontres. Mais ce congrès insiste avant tout sur le fait de conférer entre nous. Une proportion importante de votre temps se passera dans ces petits groupes de discussion. C'est de ce travail que les organisateurs attendent les principaux résultats du congrès, et non des conférences qui seront prononcées du haut de l'estrade et qui ont été conçues surtout pour orienter les discussions.

Ce congrès, qui constitue une société temporaire, comme tous les congrès, se consacre à un seul problème en particulier qui, votre présence ici l'atteste, ne reçoit pas l'attention voulue dans le cours de vos efforts quotidiens. Vous êtes ici pour discuter de l'enfance proprement dite, mais vous essayerez également de considérer un des problèmes les plus persistants, celui des rapports entre vous, le problème de se faire comprendre par delà les jargons professionnels, les disciplines et les institutions. Dans vos groupes, il vous est demandé d'expérimenter avec quelques-uns des problèmes que vous discuterez, et déjà il y a eu d'intéressants résultats hier. Ce qui s'est passé me permet de croire que vous êtes conscients d'une lutte avec vous-mêmes aussi bien qu'avec des problèmes intellectuels dont on peut mieux se détacher. La nature des discussions indique aussi qu'on se rend compte de la nécessité de scruter ses activités aussi bien que de diagnostiquer et de prescrire des remèdes pour les problèmes des autres.

Le Dr Myrdal, en nous donnant l'orientation générale de la conférence, nous a prié d'examiner quatre propositions essentielles. Elle nous a d'abord fourni un contexte plus vaste pour nos délibérations et nous a prié d'étudier les rapports entre les conditions dans lesquelles vivent nos enfants et celles dans lesquelles vivent les enfants du monde. Ensuite en discutant les années « pré-productrices », elle nous a soumis l'idée que nous traitions certains adultes comme des enfants. Voilà un contraste intéressant avec notre crainte, au Canada, que nous traitions des enfants en adultes. Voilà qui nous amène au troisième problème : « qu'est-ce qu'un enfant ? », et le Dr Myrdal a semblé suggérer que notre vocabulaire exigerait davantage de catégories qu' « enfant » et « adulte ». La dernière considération émise par notre conférencière semble répondre aux difficultés que vous avez rencontrée, dans vos groupes hier. Elle vous a indiqué deux types de réaction : imagination et compassion. Et elle a précisé que les deux étaient des réactions légitimes et nécessaires. Peut-être devrions-nous réfléchir sur notre capacité d'être à la fois imaginatifs et pleins de compassion. Nous voulons parfois tellement user de notre imagination, et apprendre aux enfants à en faire autant, que nous ne nous rendons pas compte qu'il nous faut aussi apprendre la compassion. Voilà, me semble-t-il, un peu ce qui nous est arrivé hier. Nous avons tenté de nous faire connaître et d'atteindre autrui. Nous avons tenté de faire preuve de la seule qualité qui rende la communication possible, la confiance. Si le sujet de nos discussions était important, il ne l'était pas autant que les rapports qui s'établissaient.

Il s'est également passé ce qui se passe toujours quand diverses professions se réunissent : il existe toujours une certaine rivalité sur le droit de définir le problème, chaque profession essayant de justifier son point de vue. Si l'on obtient le droit de définition, on peut alors se considérer comme spécialiste. Voilà qui est normal et nécessaire, mais aujourd'hui il nous faut nous consacrer davantage à la solution des problèmes qu'à la protection de notre sécurité grâce au statu quo.

De nombreux groupes ont parlé d'innovations et c'est à mon sens un domaine intéressant. C'est souvent en innovant que les professions se rejoignent, parce qu'en redéfinissant un problème on peut utiliser de multiples ressources sans conflit ou rivalité nocive.

En plus, ce qui s'est passé hier fait partie du débat entre ce qu'on dit qu'il faut accomplir et ce que les institutions et professions disent qu'elles peuvent ou veulent accomplir. Comme il faut faire coïncider ces deux points de vue, ce type de congrès est devenu nécessaire et important, car si l'on ne peut résoudre ce conflit, la société va trébucher, surtout une société qui a tellement investi dans la compétence technique et professionnelle. Vous avez entrepris une tâche importante et les solutions seront difficiles, mais peut-être inattendues.

Il est également intéressant de voir dans quelle mesure vous êtes prêts à relever les défis. Il y en a eu quelques sérieux jetés à la famille, à son caractère sacré, à notre dépendance d'elle. Il y a eu des changements d'attitude vis à vis de la famille. Nous parlons depuis des dizaines d'années du transfert de la responsabilité des enfants à d'autres institutions que la famille. Ce qui est nouveau, c'est la prise en charge de la famille elle-même par l'ensemble des professionnels ou par l'état. La famille, autrefois, était une collaboratrice de la société, or, c'est devenue un sujet d'études et de préoccupations.

Et il y avait beaucoup d'autres défis lancés à diverses institutions. Mais nous n'avons toutefois pas, ni à ce congrès, ni à aucun autre, à mon su, été jusqu'à mettre en doute la validité de ce qui est sans doute une de nos convictions les mieux ancrées — et les plus inconscientes : la loi sur l'éducation obligatoire. Je ne veux pas dire que c'est une erreur mais qu'il s'agit là d'une pierre angulaire de notre société qui demanderait autant d'attention que la famille.

Vous avez soulevé à maintes reprises le même problème, avec désespoir parfois : le manque de temps. Pas le temps pour un professionnel d'en écouter un autre, pas le temps d'écouter nos enfants, pas le temps de faire ce que nous savons indispensable. Je veux vous suggérer que dans ce contexte le temps est un facteur purement moral car c'est simplement ce que vous en faites. Peut-être notre désespoir reflète-t-il autre chose.

Nous vivons dans une société qui estime qu'aucun problème n'est insoluble du moment qu'on a assez de temps, assez de ressources, pour le combattre. Nous croyons que nous trouverons le remède au cancer, une cure à la plupart des maladies, si nous disposons des travaux de recherche, du temps, du personnel bien formé et des ressources matérielles nécessaires. A cause de cela, nous avons tendance à ramener le plus grand nombre de problèmes possible à des problèmes techniques, parce que c'est là que nous mettons nos espoirs. Certains de ces problèmes sont pourtant bien des problèmes d'ordre moral, auxquels il faut s'habituer, avec lesquels il faut vivre. C'est peut-être ce qu'a voulu dire le Dr Myrdal lorsqu'elle parlait du besoin de compassion. Il faut une certaine mesure de compassion pour accepter une source de souffrance et de chagrin que nous ne savons comment faire disparaître. Voilà que nous sommes encore une fois requis de faire travailler notre imagination à l'égard des problèmes techniques et notre compassion à l'égard de ceux qui ne le sont pas.

Cela m'a intéressé de voir que certaines (pas toutes) de vos discussions au sujet des jeunes enfants tendaient à se situer sur le plan technique. Elles concernaient ce que nous pourrons faire pour rendre la vie plus supportable, plus productive, pour les jeunes enfants, si nous avions des ressources suffisantes. Mais les discussions sur les adolescents étaient d'ordre moral : nous ne sommes plus aussi sûrs que le progrès technique va faire une telle différence. Peut-être est-ce parce que les enfants, en grandissant et en se rapprochant de la période pré-productrice, ne sont plus aussi dociles et se plaisent à nous défier. Nos propres doutes se reflètent davantage que dans les enfants plus jeunes. Nous ne sommes plus aussi confiants de nos capacités de traduire en langage technique les réactions des adolescents.

Parce que de nos préoccupations envers les enfants naît immédiatement une préoccupation envers nous-mêmes, nous avons exprimé un sentiment d'inquiétude vis à vis de notre responsabilité pour le monde où nos enfants grandiront. Je pense que nous devrions user de compassion à notre égard, tout comme à l'égard de ces enfants, car, après tout, nous ne sommes pas entièrement responsables du monde où nous vivons. Nous sommes le produit de plusieurs générations et quand nous parlons ce n'est pas seulement notre voix qui se fait entendre mais celle de nos pères et des pères de nos pères.

J'ai découvert, dans vos délibérations, un certain désir de cacher nos faibles à nos enfants. Et je pense qu'il serait bon de discuter entre vous dans quelle mesure nous devons leur faire partager nos difficultés. Dans ce contexte, je me suis souvenu des mots de Silone « L'ennui, avec les enfants, c'est qu'ils croient ce que leurs parents leur disent ». Il me semble que c'est là une idée très importante car nous n'entendons pas toujours ce que nous disons à nos enfants. Nous entendons ce que nous disons comme un écho à nos combats intérieurs, mais les enfants ne voient pas les combats, ils n'entendent que les mots. Voilà pourquoi, quand vous parlez de communications, il ne faut pas penser seulement aux communications entre vous mais aussi entre vous et vos enfants.

Peut-être était-ce implicite dans le regret que vous avez exprimé de ne pas voir davantage de « jeunes » présents à ce congrès.

C'est ainsi que vos discussions d'hier ont traduit trois préoccupations majeures : Que faut-il apprendre à nos enfants en tenant compte de notre propre état ? Que communiquons-nous réellement à nos enfants ? Et enfin, dans quelle mesure faut-il que nous changions pour arriver à tenir les promesses faites à nos enfants et faire quelques efforts pour les enfants dans les autres coins du monde ? Faut-il simplement nous consacrer davantage à nos tâches actuelles, ou faut-il faire certaines choses de façon différente ? Il me semble que les questions que vous vous avez posées hier, base de vos travaux d'aujourd'hui, traduisent la conscience que vous avez de devoir tomber d'accord avec l'enfant qui est en vous aussi bien qu'avec les enfants de la société au sein de laquelle nous vivons.

Roads to Maturity: Some of the Barriers

DR. M. S. RABINOVITCH

You will, I hope, have it in your hearts to forgive me for what I am about to do this morning. I have decided to play the role of gadfly. This is a conceited act and a dangerous one. It is conceited of me to presume that I can sting you into more profound and imaginative discussion. It is dangerous because people automatically lash out at gadflies. It should not surprise you that both these considerations are making me quite anxious at this moment, and that should be anxiety enough for one morning, ladies and gentlemen. But I am made even more anxious because, after listening in on your discussions yesterday, it became necessary for me to abandon the speech which I had prepared and I now stand before you with a set of random notes and a large supply of butterflies in my stomach. I shall try to ignore these and proceed with the task at hand. Essentially it is my intention to talk about sacred cows—sacred cows which may be interfering with the achievement of the goals of this conference. To begin with may I submit to you that "old cows never die, they become sacred." It is this particular type of anachronism that we must be able to discuss objectively and honestly.

The first of these sacred cows which I would offer up for scrutiny is often called professionalism. In the last two decades we have witnessed a remarkable improvement in the preparation and training of professionals who work with children, and this development is obviously desirable. We have also seen much expansion in the numbers of such professionals, and this is also desirable, indeed essential. But neither of these events has in fact resulted in adequate coverage of the needs. There are patently too few physicians, too few psychologists, too few social workers, too few nurses, dentists, and every other type of professional worker. There are not enough trained professionals to meet the needs in education, health, and welfare. It could even be said that the more professionals we train the more we seem to need. It would therefore not be surprising if this conference were to conclude that what is required is a great increase in the number of professionally trained people in the fields of health, welfare, and education. It would not be surprising. It would be easy. It would be pointless: a waste of the effort and money and time that have gone into the preparation and execution of this conference.

May I submit to you, ladies and gentlemen, that this kind of thinking does in fact constitute a barrier to the achievement of our aims. Training is important and desirable. Professionals are important and desirable. But I cannot honestly believe that there will ever be enough professionals with enough training to do the work which needs doing. To sit around and bemoan the shortage of professionals is a waste of time.

It seems to me that with the expansion of the professions there has grown up an attitude of professionalism. "To thine own profession be true—to thine own agency be true—[and lately] to thy professional trade union be true." There is nothing intrinsically wrong with this attitude. But it does carry with it the grave danger that with the pressure for protecting the trade-union interests of the professions we will lose sight of the interests of children. There is the grave danger that the philosophy of protecting the public through allowing only certified professionals to deal with the public is really becoming a philosophy of protecting the professionals themselves and providing these professionals with bargaining power at the negotiating tables.

Should we not be concerned with the question of how this kind of "closed-shop" mentality influences the availability of desperately needed services? If, as many have pointed out, it will not be possible to provide the staggering numbers of highly trained professionals that, according to our present ways of thinking, are needed; if it is less than completely honest to continue to use this type of reasoning solely as the wedge to obtain more and more training facilities—are we not duty bound to think of new ways to meet the needs? Are we not duty bound to examine very carefully the details of what we do in order to evaluate the possibility that much of our effort is directed to activities that could be done as well, or even better, by people with less training? Is it not possible that the qualifications for membership in professional organizations are not synonymous with the qualifications for doing the specific jobs that many of us are doing? Is it possible that, by virtue of our closed shop attitudes, we are preventing others from doing these jobs? Rather than sit around and cry about the shortage of professionals, might we not use our time more constructively by devising new ways to mobilize new manpower?

It may be that highly trained professionals must accept as one of their major responsibilities the training of able housewives to become a large, service-oriented, task force. Perhaps the professionals must train those able women whose families are now grown independent and who are searching for meaningful activities. I am not here referring to volunteers, but rather to trained personnel. Not overtrained personnel, but people trained, perhaps in the actual service settings, to do specific jobs that need doing. In some settings these sub-professional personnel might require six months of training, while in other settings it could be that a training period of twice that duration is appropriate.

One hears much now about the problems associated with the increase in leisure time, of how increasing automation will result in many more people, men and women, with more non-job time on their hands. Perhaps it is time to plan for at least some of this non-job time to be directed into semi-professional activities in the fields of health, welfare, and education. It may well be that this is indeed the only possible way to deal with the man-power needs of the helping professions. Would it be possible to encourage people with shrinking job-time to undertake training for second jobs and to work with professionals in health, education, and welfare services? It seems reasonable that any objective assessment of these possibilities requires that we first break away from any narrow professionalism that may have crept into our attitudes, and then use our imaginations freely and extensively in working out ways of meeting the man-power demands with which we are daily confronted.

I would like now to go on to the second sacred cow. This one is called "the family." If there has been moaning and groaning about the shortage of professionals, there has surely been a lot more moaning and groaning about the state of the family. There has, in my estimation, been a great deal of sentimental, romantic, and sanctimonious talk about the family. It is my intention to urge you to examine the institution of the family with dispassionate and penetrating vision, because it seems that only objective, hard-boiled scrutiny is likely to lead to steps that will eventually result in desirable improvements.

I would not claim my experience to be completely representative, but it has often struck me that many of the people who are most vocal on the subject of the family, who wish for the good old days, are people who do not have families. I mean by this that there is a Pollyanna-like quality, an emotional up-in-the-clouds quality, about their statements. They sound blissfully unaware that family living is difficult. It is difficult for children and for parents. And it may be getting more difficult all the time. It is not enough to make proclamations about the good family any more than it is good enough to make proclamations against sin and for motherhood. It is more and more the case that people are being educated to get along technically and interpersonally at their place of work. Where is one to learn about the infinitely more difficult, more complex, and more important ways of living constructively and with satisfactions in a family. If a man's work week were abruptly reduced and it became necessary that he spend ten or twenty more hours each week with his family, this would present a real problem. It would require some hard thinking and careful planning if that additional time was to be constructive and satisfying to all concerned.

Many of you are by now saying to yourselves that the place to learn about family life is by living in a family. Surely we all learned this as children growing up in families. There are difficulties with this. The family I grew up in is different from the family my wife and I have created. There may have been a time when the living patterns of one generation were similar and continuous with the living patterns of the generation immediately following. This is not really the case now. The rate of change seems to have been stepped up and the immediate consequence of this is that growing up in a family may not contribute as much as we imagine, or hope, towards learning how to create and organize a family of your own. The old folks pine for the values, the good things, that we choose to remember from our youth. But this is surely as useless as it is understandable.

How much do children learn from books, from television, from the families of their friends? We really don't know how children learn about family life. We don't know how much a child is influenced by his own family compared with the effect of forces outside the family. We want children to acquire the "good" values which we assume are available in their family settings. But we have precious little knowledge about the values that in fact are available in their families. And we have even less knowledge about how to actually teach, or at least encourage learning about, the values that we might want the child to acquire. It is not pious statements about the great worth of the family that we need, but knowledge about how people can, through family life achieve satisfying emotional experiences which will have some enduring qualities. Perhaps we need to examine carefully what values can in fact be learned in the modern family structure and what ones can no longer be acquired naturally in that environment.

One frequently is asked the question "How can parents put character into children?" This may be the wrong question. Perhaps the more realistic one is "How do you give children the opportunity to extract character out of their environment and make it part of themselves, and what are the aspects of their environment that are most appropriate for these purposes?" The family is, increasingly, only one of these aspects. Sentimental and wishy-washy feelings about the family are not conducive to the increase in knowledge that we desperately require.

I should like to take a few more moments to pursue this particular sacred cow into one specific area. One example of the sentimental family notion as a barrier to effective action has been the situation of the so-called multi-problem family. We as a society accept various compulsory conditions which are in fact invasions of privacy and interfere with individual rights; vaccinations, compulsory education, laws which prohibit suicide and drug addiction, and, more recently, provisions which enable the state to enforce necessary medical treatment even against the wishes of parents. We accept these principles, which are contrary to the principles of individual rights, because of the notion of the welfare of the group. But many of us turn soft at the prospect of compulsion applied to family situations, particularly the prospect of breaking up families, separating parents from children. Most people when told that two individuals have dissolved their marriage react by saying "too bad" or words to that effect. Surely that is jumping to an unwarranted conclusion.

The dilemma here is particularly apparent in the case of the multi-problem family. There is considerable evidence that such families perpetuate themselves and their problems. They cost the community a great deal of money and cause many innocent people much heartache. The children reared in such families are very likely to continue the pattern set by their parents. Medicine long ago learned to deal with infectious diseases by first isolating the victim from the source of infection. To follow this plan and prevent the spread of infectious social diseases by the multi-problem family requires isolating the children from their parents and from the environment which has given rise to the condition. But, I hear the cry welling up: "even a bad family is better than no family." Surely this is not meant seriously! Surely the people who say this are not familiar with what it is like to live in one of those families. Surely these people are projecting the experience of their own family life, albeit slightly sullied, and are not aware of the living hell it is to be a helpless child or a helpless adult trapped in the vicious, dehumanizing, never-ending morass that is life in some family situations. Such situations constitute social malignancy and often require "radical surgery." It seems to me that what we are really saying is that "even a bad family is better than a bad institution, or a bad foster home, or a succession of questionable foster homes." We might feel very differently about forcing family separations if there were better institutions, better and many more individual as well as group foster homes, to which children could be sent while some attempt is being made to change the parents and their environment. And if such changes were not possible, the child might still do much better growing up in a good institution than in a destructive family.

It may well be that the principle involved here goes beyond the instances of obvious and severe social malignancy. One is confronted by the problem of chipping away at the principles of freedom for the individual, by the basic question of whether any principles can or should forever remain unchanged despite changing conditions and changing attitudes.

I would like now to proceed to another barrier, another sacred cow in our midst. I refer to the notion so many people have of the child as a miniature adult; or childhood as a sort of way-station on the road to adulthood. Many of us, I am sure, have had the experience, when we were little, of the adult who says "well now, my son, what do you want to be when you grow up?" This is not really a terribly intelligent question to pose to a six-year-old or even a twelve-year-old. But more important, it is a demeaning question. It says to "my son" that what he is now, or what he wants to be today is quite unimportant. It is only the long-range goal that has virtue. Childhood is a necessary evil, and the sooner you have done with it "my son," the better.

It is not difficult to understand this attitude. Not so very long ago most young people entered the labour market at sixteen or seventeen years of age and began to create families soon after. It was necessary to be prepared for adulthood, in the productive sense, soon after puberty. However, today, such an attitude is anachronistic. On a chronological scale the age of puberty is being pushed closer to childhood and the age of productive (job) adulthood is being pushed in the opposite direction. It is becoming increasingly difficult to treat this extended period of growing up as a period of marking time, a period which many of us seem to assume has no intrinsic virtues of its own. There is less and less need now to plan job training when a child is nine years of age. For more and more children there is the opportunity to spend many years in pre-productive activities; fewer and fewer teenagers will be required to enter the labour market. We may be on the threshold of a wonderful opportunity to really let children be children and young adults be young adults. We may now have the opportunity on an increasing scale, to explore and enrich the joys and passions associated with each phase of growth and development: to enrich the joy in "discovery," the hallmark of childhood; to enrich the vital and passionate sense of "justice," the hallmark of the young adult. We actually may have more time in which to encourage the development of desirable adult patterns of behaviour, and also have the time to encourage children and youth to make the most of their pre-productive years. This will require some changes. Our present social structures are strained. This is particularly evident in our relatively poor ability to provide stimulating and constructive experiences for young adults. We will need to be imaginative and resourceful, and be prepared to admit to our own errors. I am most interested in the alternatives proposed by Madame Myrdal. She spoke of creating villages or sub-cities for young adults where they could live, and work, and learn; social structures which would allow young adults to express and develop their personalities without the frequent clashes which we now witness between the young adult and the older adult both competing in the same arena. She also spoke of direct wages to youth who are at school so as to modify the present version of dependency. We have tried to keep them down and it does not work very well. Perhaps it is time to try another approach.

And now the last of the sacred cows about which I will talk this morning. This one is difficult to give a single name. Our frequent lament is that times are changing so rapidly that we do not know for what type of world to prepare our children. "Let us try to make them ready for anything and leave it at that." This is surely nonsense! We know that the population of the world is predominantly "coloured": the largest nations of the world are not white, do not have our ideas of political democracy and personal freedoms, do not have our type of economic organization, but will soon have our technology. Our children will have to co-exist, at home and abroad, without the arrogance which has until now typified our attitude of western white superiority. Future historians will decide whether it will have proved harder to "liberalize the communist régimes or to socialize the western ones."

I submit to you that we know enough now to plan in at least three general areas. We know enough to plan for individual and group responsibility, and to foster and nourish the quest for knowledge.

Our children will need to know how to live with themselves. They will exist in an increasingly welfare-oriented state; an environment in which the risk of becoming a robot will be ever present; an environment in which some degree of self-determination will be the reward of those who work hard for it. They will need to learn how to have some independence of mind, of spirit, and of action, within the context of a society which could easily slip into patterns of perceiving such independence as a threat. The more numerous such independent, responsible people, the less likely that our society will in fact destroy the free spirit. We must surely place before our children living examples of such free, yet responsible, people. We must encourage open discussion of the problems which we face, the problems of individuality and the problems of group welfare. Our youth should be encouraged to learn by participation about the numerous and complex issues faced by our society.

A second, and obviously related, area about which we know enough to plan, is that of group, or more precisely, inter-group, responsibility. Our children will live in a world in which getting along with people of different language, different colour, different economic ideology, different moral ideology will be more real for them than for us. Their ability to achieve co-existence may well be the major factor in whether our particular values, however modified, persist or whether our way of life is forcibly replaced by others. We must teach our children that what is happening just four or six jet hours away is of concern to us. Surely we want our children to know about and to experience other cultures, other languages, other economic systems. Surely we must begin to create concrete ways for our youth to meet and live with the new diversity that will increasingly characterize life on this planet. This can and must happen in our cities, in our provinces, in our country, and in our world.

The third, and last, point I wish to discuss has to do with the quest for knowledge: the joy of exploration, of discovery, of innovation; the adventure of knowing things, the adventure of unravelling the mysteries of this universe. It seems to me that children come into this world with a considerable drive to learn and thereby to understand and control their environment. At all times and in all places man has worked at the accumulation of knowledge and the mastery of his surroundings. Perhaps this is what the man meant when in response to the question "Why did you climb Mount Everest?" he replied, "Because it was there." We may not envy the actual climb, but we should envy the spirit, the gumption, and the singleminded dedication that is symbolized in that adventure. It may be that over and above humanitarian motivations the medical scientist struggles to conquer disease because it is there, and the physical scientist works to reach the moon, and then Mars, and then Jupiter, because they are there, not because of prestige or because of the arms race. The pace at which these discoveries take place seems to be influenced by many things, but the fact that these drives to know more are there, and always have been there, cannot be attributed to the East-West struggle. We know that man is distinguished from other animals by his quest for new knowledge, new ideas, and new ways to solve old problems. What we do not yet know as well is how to nurture this drive into productive adulthood. We can admire the marvellous advances of the physical sciences and engineering. We need to do much to match them in the social sciences and the helping professions.

Quelques obstacles sur les chemins de la maturité

J'ESPÈRE que vous aurez la générosité de me pardonner ce que je vais faire ce matin, car j'ai l'intention de me transformer en gros bourdon ! Voilà qui est à la fois prétentieux et dangereux. Quelle prétention ! Croire que je peux vous aiguillonner et vous inspirer des discussions originales et profondes ! De plus, les gens, automatiquement, essayent de détruire le gros bourdon. Il n'est donc pas surprenant que je ressente une certaine anxiété ce matin. Et comme si ça ne suffisait pas, après vous avoir écouté hier, j'ai dû abandonner la conférence que j'avais préparée. Me voilà maintenant avec quelques notes, rédigées très vite, et des palpitations. Mais, en dépit d'elles, j'aborderai le corps du sujet. Je veux avant tout vous parler de vaches sacrées, de ces vaches sacrées qui risquent de compromettre les buts que s'est fixé ce congrès. Pour commencer, j'énoncerai le principe que « les vieilles vaches ne meurent jamais; elles deviennent sacrées ». Et je veux consacrer cet exposé à cet animal. C'est de ce type particulier d'anachronisme qu'il nous faut discuter avec objectivité et honnêteté.

La première des vaches sacrées que je veux disséquer, c'est ce qu'on pourrait appeler le professionnalisme. Au cours des vingt dernières années, nous avons pu voir un progrès remarquable se produire dans la formation des professionnels qui se consacrent à l'enfance, et c'est très bien. Nous avons vu également augmenter considérablement le nombre des professionnels, ce qui est essentiel. Mais malgré tout, on n'a pas réussi à répondre à tous les besoins : il y a trop peu de médecins, trop peu de psychologues, de travailleurs sociaux, d'infirmières, trop peu de dentistes et autres professionnels, en fonction de tous les besoins existant dans les domaines de la santé, du bien-être et de l'éducation. On pourrait même dire que, plus nous formons de professionnels, plus nous en avons besoin. Il n'y aurait donc rien d'étonnant si ce congrès arrive à la conclusion que ce qu'il faut, c'est augmenter considérablement le nombre des professionnels dans ces trois domaines. Cela n'aurait rien de surprenant, ce serait facile. Et cela ne servirait à rien : ce serait gaspiller les efforts, le temps et l'argent investis dans la préparation de ce congrès. Puis-je vous suggérer que cette façon de penser est, en fait, un obstacle à nos buts ? La formation est nécessaire, importante. Les professionnels sont nécessaires, importants. Mais je ne peux pas croire qu'il y en aura jamais assez pour suffire à la tâche. C'est perdre son temps que de gémir sur leur nombre insuffisant.

Il me semble qu'avec l'expansion des professions est née l'attitude que je qualifierai de « professionalisme »... « Sois fidèle à ta profession, sois fidèle à ton agence et [plus récemment] sois fidèle à ton syndicat ». Cette attitude n'a rien de répréhensible, intrinsèquement, mais elle est potentiellement dangereuse, parce que nous essayons de protéger les intérêts des syndicats et nous oublions les intérêts des enfants. Il existe un grave danger, celui de voir la protection qu'on assure au public en ne laissant que des professionnels agréés s'occuper de lui dégénérer en protection des professionnels eux-mêmes, qui ont obtenu jusqu'au droit de marchandage. Il me semble qu'il faudrait nous préoccuper un peu de la façon dont cette mentalité de clocher va affecter la possibilité de fournir aux enfants les services dont ils ont tant besoin. S'il ne devient jamais possible, comme beaucoup l'ont fait remarquer, d'obtenir le nombre écrasant de professionnels avec une formation très poussée dont, suivant notre point de vue actuel, nous avons besoin ; si ce n'est pas complètement honnête d'utiliser ce type de raisonnement simplement comme une arme pour créer de plus en plus de possibilités de formation, est-ce que nous ne devrions pas chercher de nouvelles méthodes pour faire face aux besoins ? N'est-ce pas un devoir que d'étudier soigneusement et en détail tout ce que nous faisons pour évaluer si, dans une large mesure, nos activités ne pourraient pas être accomplies aussi bien, sinon mieux, par des gens moins formés ? N'est-il pas possible que ce qu'on exige des candidats aux organisations professionnelles coïncide avec ce que nous, ou la plupart d'entre nous, accomplissons chaque jour, ou, qu'en raison de notre mentalité de clocher, nous empêchons les autres d'accomplir ? Au lieu de nous asseoir et de nous désoler du manque de professionnels, ne pourrions-nous pas réfléchir aux moyens de mobiliser un nouveau type de collaborateurs ? N'appartient-il pas aux professionnels qui bénéficient d'une formation intense de former, par exemple, des maîtresses de maison qui en sont capables et d'en faire un groupe vraiment orienté vers les services ? Ou encore éduquer les femmes dont les enfants ont grandi et quitté la maison et qui cherchent autour d'elles quelque chose d'intéressant à faire ? Je ne parle pas ici de volontaires, mais de personnel qualifié. Pas super-formé, simplement formé, peut-être même au cours de stages pratiques. Dans certains cas, il peut falloir six mois de formation, dans d'autres, le double au moins.

On parle beaucoup en ce moment des problèmes que soulève l'augmentation des loisirs, de la façon dont l'automation laissera à un grand nombre d'hommes et de femmes du temps libre. Peut-être est-il temps de s'organiser pour qu'une partie au moins de ces loisirs se transforment en activités semi-professionnelles dans les domaines de la santé, de l'éducation et du bien-être. Il se pourrait bien que ce soit le seul moyen de trouver les travailleurs dont on a besoin pour aider les professionnels. Serait-il possible d'encourager les gens dont les horaires de travail diminuent à entreprendre les études nécessaires pour avoir un deuxième emploi qui les ferait travailler aux côtés des spécialistes dans les services de santé, d'éducation et de bien-être ? Il semble raisonnable que toute évaluation objective de ces possibilités exige de nous avant tout que nous abandonnions tout professionnalisme dans nos attitudes et que nous usions de notre imagination librement pour trouver des façons de suppléer au manque de personnel auquel nous devons faire face quotidiennement.

J'aimerais m'en prendre maintenant à ma deuxième vache sacrée : elle a pour nom « la famille ». Si l'on soupire et gémit en parlant des professionnels, combien plus on a gémi et soupiré en parlant de la famille. A mon avis on en a parlé bien trop sentimentalement, romantiquement et vertueusement. Et j'ai l'intention de vous inviter à examiner l'institution de la famille avec calme et pénétration, parce qu'il semble bien que seule une étude froide et objective peut nous amener à prendre les mesures qui finalement permettront les améliorations nécessaires.

Je ne prétends pas que mes expériences soient absolument typiques, mais il me semble que la plupart des gens qui se lamentent sur l'état de la famille et parlent du bon vieux temps sont des gens sans famille. Ils s'expriment avec un optimisme débordant, la tête dans les nuages, et ils ne semblent pas se douter que la vie de famille est difficile. Difficile pour les enfants et difficile pour les parents. Ça ne suffit pas de parler de la vraie famille, pas plus qu'il ne suffit de se proclamer contre le péché et pour l'amour maternel. Nous apprenons de plus en plus aux gens comment se comporter vis-à-vis de leur travail et avec leurs collaborateurs, mais où peut-on apprendre la technique infiniment plus difficile, plus délicate et plus complexe de vivre de façon constructive et enrichissante au sein d'une famille ? Si la semaine de travail d'un homme raccourcit brusquement et s'il lui faut passer de dix à vingt heures de plus chaque semaine avec sa famille, un réel problème peut se poser. Il faudrait mûre réflexion et organisation minutieuse pour rendre ces heures fructueuses pour tous.

Bon nombre d'entre vous se disent en ce moment que l'endroit idéal où apprendre à vivre en famille... c'est la famille. Sûrement nous avons tous appris, enfants, en grandissant au milieu d'une famille. En bien ça n'est pas aussi simple que ça. La famille où j'ai grandi n'est pas la même que celle que ma femme et moi avons fondée. A une certaine époque, les modes de vie ont pu être similaires d'une génération à l'autre, et il y a pu avoir continuité entre une génération et la suivante. Il n'en est plus ainsi. Les changements arrivent de plus en plus rapidement, et la conséquence immédiate en est qu'avoir vécu, enfant, au sein d'une famille, n'aide pas autant que nous l'imaginons à nous préparer à fonder notre propre famille. Nous, les vieux, nous regrettons les valeurs, les belles choses que nous choisissons de nous rappeler du temps de notre jeunesse. C'est évidemment aussi inutile que normal.

Dans quelle mesure les enfants apprennent-ils de la maison, de la télévision ou des familles de leurs amis ? Nous ignorons en réalité comment les enfants apprennent la vie de famille. Nous ne savons pas combien l'enfant est influencé par sa propre famille, et par les influences extérieures. Nous voulons que les enfants acquièrent le sens des valeurs qu'ils trouvent dans leur famille, pensons-nous. Mais, en fait, nous ne savons pas grand chose des valeurs qui prédominent dans les familles. Et nous savons encore moins comment enseigner ou du moins encourager l'apprentissage des valeurs que nous voudrions que l'enfant acquière. Et ce ne sont pas de pieuses remarques sur la beauté de la famille dont nous avons besoin, mais de connaissances sur la façon dont les individus peuvent faire de la vie familiale une série d'expériences affectives, enrichissantes, dont les résultats seront durables. Peut-être faudrait-il étudier avec soin quelles valeurs peuvent en fait s'apprendre dans le cadre de la famille moderne, et quelles valeurs ne s'y découvrent plus.

On se voit souvent poser la question « Comment les parents peuvent-ils former le caractère de leurs enfants » ? C'est peut-être la mauvaise question. Peut-être la bonne question serait : « comment peut-on aider les enfants à se former le caractère à partir du milieu où ils vivent, et quels sont les éléments du milieu les mieux susceptibles de jouer ce rôle » ? Les familles de plus en plus ne représentent qu'un seul de ces éléments. Les beaux sentiments à l'égard de la famille ne nous aideront pas à acquérir les connaissances dont nous avons désespérément besoin.

Puis-je me permettre de continuer encore un peu ma chasse à la vache sacrée « famille » et cela, dans un domaine tout spécial. Un bon exemple de concept sentimental, qui se dresse comme un obstacle à l'action efficace, c'est la situation de ce qu'on a baptisé la « famille à problèmes multiples ». En tant que société nous acceptons des obligations variées qui sont en fait une violation de l'intimité et qui attaquent les droits de l'individu : vaccinations, éducation obligatoire, lois interdisant le suicide et la narcomanie, et, plus récemment, lois permettant à l'état d'imposer des soins médicaux à un enfant contre le gré des parents. Nous acceptions tout cela, qui est contraire au principe des droits sacrés de l'individu, à cause du concept de bien public. Mais la plupart d'entre nous manquent totalement d'enthousiasme devant l'idée d'intervention de force dans des situations familiales : familles séparées, enfants retirés aux parents, etc. La plupart des gens, quand on leur dit que deux individus ont dissout leur mariage, s'exclament : « Quel dommage ! » Sûrement c'est là conclure un peu vite.

Le dilemme est particulièrement visible quand il s'agit de la famille à problèmes multiples. Il existe un nombre de faits qui suggèrent que de telles familles se perpétuent et perpétuent leurs problèmes. Elles coûtent cher à la société, et font souffrir bien des innocents. Les enfants élevés dans de telles familles ont toutes les chances de continuer sur le chemin tracé par les parents. La médecine a appris il y a longtemps que le meilleur moyen de traiter une maladie infectieuse, c'est d'isoler la victime de la source de l'infection. Pour suivre cette méthode et empêcher que ne se répande l'infection des maladies sociales par la famille à problèmes multiples, il faudrait isoler les enfants du milieu et des parents. Mais j'entends déjà le cri familier : « Mieux vaut une famille déplorable que pas de famille du tout ». Sûrement ça n'est pas sérieux. Sûrement les gens qui disent cela ne savent pas ce que c'est que de vivre dans une de ces familles. Sûrement ces gens projettent leur expérience familiale, un peu dénaturée, et ne se rendent pas compte de l'enfer que peut être la vie pour un enfant ou un adulte sans défense pris au piège dans ce marécage vicieux, inhumain et sans espoir. De telles situations sont de véritables cancers, qui exigent le scalpel du chirurgien. Il me semble que ce que nous voulons réellement dire, c'est « Mieux vaut une famille déplorable qu'une institution déplorable, qu'une famille adoptive déplorable ou qu'une succession de foyers adoptifs médiocres ». Nous réagirions peut-être différemment à l'idée de la séparation des enfants et des parents si nous avions de meilleures institutions, de meilleurs et bien plus nombreux foyers adoptifs, individuels ou de groupe, où l'on pourrait envoyer l'enfant tandis qu'on s'efforcerait de changer la famille et le milieu. Et si le changement s'avérait impossible, l'enfant aurait meilleur compte à grandir dans une bonne institution que dans une famille destructive.

Il est bien possible que le principe en cause ne s'applique pas seulement aux cancers sociaux les plus visibles. On se trouve confronté par le problème des petites entailles aux droits de l'individu, par la question de savoir si un principe doit rester immuable ou s'il doit évoluer avec les conditions et les attitudes.

J'aimerais maintenant passer à un autre obstacle, une autre vache sacrée dans nos murs. Je veux parler de l'idée que tant de gens se font de l'enfant : un adulte en miniature, et de l'enfance : une sorte de voie de garage sur le chemin de la maturité. Nous avons tous, je pense, entendu dans notre enfance, un adulte nous demander : « Alors, mon fils, qu'est-ce que tu feras quand tu seras grand » ? Ça n'est pas une question très intelligente à poser à un enfant de six ans, ou même de onze ou douze ans. Mais c'est surtout une question humiliante. Cela veut dire à « mon fils » que ce qu'il est, que ce qu'il veut être aujourd'hui n'a aucune importance. Ce qui compte c'est le but lointain. L'enfance est un mal nécessaire et le plus tôt que tu en auras fini, « mon fils », le mieux ce sera.

Il n'est pas difficile de comprendre cette attitude. Il n'y a pas si longtemps les jeunes gens de seize ou dix-sept ans entraient dans le monde des travailleurs et presque tout de suite fondaient un foyer. Il leur fallait donc se préparer à la vie adulte au sens de « productivité » dès la puberté. Mais aujourd'hui une telle conception est un anachronisme. Sur le plan chronologique, l'âge de la puberté est déplacé vers l'enfance, et l'âge adulte productif (emploi) est déplacé dans le sens inverse. Il devient de plus en plus difficile de considérer cette période prolongée de la croissance comme un période d'attente, une période qui semble pour la plupart d'entre nous n'avoir aucune qualité intrinsèque. Il est de moins en moins nécessaire de préparer la carrière d'un enfant quand il a neuf ans. Un nombre sans cesse croissant d'enfants ont la possibilité de passer de plus en plus de temps à des activités « pré-productives ». De moins en moins on attend des adolescents qu'ils se fassent une place sur le marché du travail. Peut-être pourrons-nous bientôt laisser, ô merveille, les enfants être des enfants et les jeunes adultes être des jeunes adultes. Nous aurons peut-être la possibilité d'explorer et d'enrichir davantage les joies et les passions de chaque étape de la croissance : enrichir la joie de la découverte, caractéristique de l'enfance ; enrichir le sens vital et passionné de la justice, caractéristique du jeune adulte. Nous avons réellement davantage de temps pour encourager le développement de types de conduite adulte souhaitables et nous avons aussi le temps d'encourager les enfants et les jeunes à retirer le maximum de ces années pré-productives. Il faudra pour cela effectuer certains changements. Les structures sociales sont trop tendues. Cela se remarque particulièrement dans la façon relativement médiocre dont nous arrivons à fournir aux jeunes adultes des expériences stimulantes et constructives. Il nous faudra de l'imagination et des ressources, et être prêts à admettre nos propres erreurs. J'ai été très intéressé par les suggestions de Mme Myrdal. Elle a proposé de bâtir des villages, de petites cités pour les jeunes adultes, où ils pourraient vivre, travailler, apprendre. Des structures sociales qui permettraient au jeune adulte de s'exprimer, de développer sa personnalité sans les heurts fréquents dont nous sommes témoins entre le jeune adulte et l'adulte plus âgé, rivalisant dans le même domaine. Elle a également parlé de salaires directement payés aux jeunes, quand ils poursuivent leurs études, afin de modifier leur situation de dépendance. Nous avons essayé de les restreindre, et ça ne marche pas. Il est peut-être temps de s'y prendre autrement.

Et maintenant, la dernière des vaches sacrées. Du moins la dernière à laquelle je m'attaquerai ce matin. Il est difficile du lui trouver un nom précis. Notre lamentation presque quotidienne est que la marche du temps est si rapide que nous ne savons pas à quelle sorte de vie il convient de préparer nos enfants. « Essayons de les préparer à tout et n'en parlons plus ». Quelle sottise ! Nous savons que le monde est constitué surtout de gens de couleur, que les plus grandes nations du monde ne sont pas de race blanche, ne partagent pas nos idées sur la démocratie, n'ont pas notre sentiment vis-à-vis de la liberté individuelle, ne possèdent pas notre type d'organisation économique, mais auront bientôt notre technologie. Nos enfants devront coexister ici et à l'étranger, sans manifester l'arrogance qu'inspirait jusqu'ici notre sentiment de la supériorité de l'Occidental blanc. Les historiens de l'avenir auront à décider s'il est plus difficile de libéraliser le régime communiste ou de socialiser le monde occidental.

Je veux vous soumettre le principe que nous en savons assez pour nous préparer au moins dans trois domaines. Nous en savons assez pour travailler dans le domaine de la responsabilité individuelle, dans celui de la responsabilité collective, et nous pouvons faire naître et encourager la recherche du savoir. Nos enfants auront besoin de savoir comment vivre avec eux-mêmes. Ils vivront dans un monde de plus en plus organisé, dans un mileu où les risques de devenir un robot sont toujours présents. Un milieu dans lequel un certain degré d'autonomie sera la récompense de celui qui y consacrera des efforts suivis. Nos enfants devront apprendre comment acquérir une certaine indépendance d'action et d'esprit, dans le contexte d'une société qui pourrait facilement en venir à considérer une telle indépendance comme une menace.

Plus il existera de ces gens indépendants et conscients de leurs responsabilités et moins la société détruira la liberté de l'esprit. Nous devons placer sous les yeux de nos enfants des exemples de ces gens libres mais qui font face à leurs responsabilités. Nous devons encourager la libre discussion des problèmes que nous rencontrons, problèmes de personnalité, problèmes de bien-être public. Il faut encourager la jeunesse à s'informer, en y participant, de tous les problèmes complexes auxquels notre société doit faire face.

Un autre domaine, qui y est évidemment relié, dans lequel nos connaissances sont suffisantes pour que nous puissions organiser et nous préparer, c'est celui des responsabilités de groupes ou plus précisément inter-groupes. Les enfants vivront dans un monde où ils devront côtoyer et s'entendre avec des gens de langue différente, de couleur différente, d'idéologie différente, de morale différente. Toutes ces différences seront plus réelles pour eux que pour nous. Leur capacité de coexister pourrait bien être le facteur essentiel permettant de déterminer si nos valeurs propres peuvent persister, même modifiées, ou si notre mode de vie doit être remplacé, de force, par un autre. Nous devons apprendre à nos enfants que ce qui se passe à 4 ou 6 heures de réacté a de l'importance. Nous voulons sûrement que nos enfants connaissent d'autres cultures, d'autres langues, d'autres systèmes économiques. Nous devons trouver des moyens concrets de faire participer notre jeunesse à toute cette diversité qui devient de plus en plus la caractéristique de notre planète. Tout cela peut se faire dans nos villes, dans nos provinces, dans notre pays, dans notre monde.

Le troisième point que je veux enfin aborder, c'est la quête du savoir. La joie de l'exploration, de la découverte, de l'innovation. L'aventure de la connaissance, l'aventure de la solution enfin apportée aux mystères de l'univers. Il me semble que les enfants naissent avec la soif de savoir, par conséquent de comprendre et dominer leur milieu. Toujours et partout, l'homme a travaillé à amasser des connaissances et à maîtriser son entourage. Peut-être c'est là ce que voulait dire celui qui répondait, quand on lui demandait pourquoi il avait escaladé l'Everest « Parce qu'il était là ». Peut être n'envions-nous pas l'ascension elle même, mais nous envions le cran, l'énergie, l'opiniâtreté que symbolise cet exploit. Il se peut que, au délà des motivations humanitaires, le chercheur médical lutte contre la maladie parce qu'elle est là, le physicien tente de gagner la lune, et Mars, et Jupiter, parce qu'ils sont là, et non pas pour la gloire ou pour gagner la course aux armements. Le rythme auquel se font ces découvertes semble influencé par bien des choses, mais le fait que cette soif de savoir est là, qu'elle a toujours été là, n'a rien à faire avec la lutte entre l'Orient et l'Occident. Nous savons que ce qui distingue l'homme de l'animal c'est cette quête du savoir, de nouvelles idées, de solutions neuves à de vieux problèmes. Ce que nous ne savons pas encore, c'est comment entretenir cette soif pour servir un âge adulte productif. Nous pouvons bien admirer les progrès remarquables des sciences physiques et mécaniques ; il reste beaucoup à faire pour arriver aux mêmes résultats dans le domaine des sciences sociales et des services.

Review and Commentary: II

DR. ALAN THOMAS

ANYONE LISTENING to your deliberations yesterday would realize that when you discussed children you discussed the whole world. At one pole was the belief that the nurture and proper care of children is the responsibility of the total society all of the time; at the other pole that this responsibility could be delegated to specialists. The problem of whether in reality there was a choice and if so on what grounds it could be made and the implications of the choice concerned many. Your discussions yesterday and my comments about them can be summarized under the general categories established by Dr. Rabinovitch in his presentation.

In the field of values, some of your groups were concerned about the nature of our society and its responsibility, whether direct or delegated, for the nurture of children. In this context you discussed problems of automation, of leisure, of poverty, which are general social problems which affect children as well as adults. And there was an indication that some of you had been listening to the young and had found that possibly they were learning to deal with these problems more quickly and with greater agility than we were. Some of you were reflecting on what the young are telling us about how to deal with a society of many choices and in which there is a great deal more freedom than anything we have experienced. Much practical discussion and a good deal of interest centred on the nature, purpose, and achievements of Operation Headstart in the United States.

From your discussion of some of the professional groups to whom we have delegated some specific responsibilities, it was obvious that Dr. Rabinovitch's address had triggered a great deal of concern. When we are dealing with professionalism we are dealing with problems of knowledge and power in our society. You tangled, in a number of groups, with the problem of what constitutes being a "professional." Is it just being extremely competent at one's job or are there other responsibilities and privileges? This it seemed to me was a very fruitful area of discussion for it raised again the issue of the delegation of responsibility and how realistic this may be and what responsibilities we have, as a society, for professional development and professional behaviour. Perhaps this discussion was most useful in the frequency with which groups dealt with volunteers and the relationship between volunteers and professionals.

This led, in several groups, to mention of the shortage of time available for training and supervising volunteers which many professionals have experienced, and to a plea for a redefinition of the professional's role and the responsibility which he must carry if more and more people are to perform some kind of function within his area of specialization. This, it seems to me, is an enormously useful area of discussion because in recent times the demand for more ability, for more intelligence has increased dramatically and we are having to re-examine what a professional is and what role he should play in society.

The schools were a frequent focus of discussion and there was an ambivalence about whether, on the one hand, the school could perform satisfactorily all that was being required of it and, on the other, whether they should not be doing far more. There was some very frank discussion and one could hear some possibilities for the inter-communication between different professional groups which we had acknowledged as one of our most pressing problems.

Many groups also wrestled with the very difficult problem raised by Dr. Rabinovitch regarding the use of force or compulsion and acknowledged that areas of freedom change in any society and that we may have to face the acceptance of less freedom of choice in the future in some areas.

Concern was aroused in many groups and there were strong and varied reactions to Dr. Rabinovitch's comments about family and "sacred cows." Some of you felt that there was nothing wrong with the family as we know it, it simply needed to be helped and strengthened. Others felt that the function of the family was changing and that we must be able to respond to the notion of change without losing touch with the essential institution. There was an uneasy discussion, in some groups, about the intervention of compulsion and whether this would challenge and weaken the integrity of the family.

Underlying much of the discussion of the family was the question of establishing contact with the family. Where is it that society reaches the family? How many areas of contact can be identified? Are there points where society can reach the family before break-down has occurred? Are there any that are potentially preventive rather than only therapeutic?

It seems to me that this problem of "force" is one that requires sensitive discussion. For example, there seemed to be a very active interest in the compulsory provision of family-life education but much of the discussion seemed to imply that we, the experts, could tell families how to do something. My professional bias would lead me to suggest that, from the point of view of adult education, this is fraught with dangers and that we must engage in some type of mutual learning if we are to succeed.

With respect to the process yesterday, it seemed to me that most of you found discussion more difficult and painful. This was, perhaps, to be expected because the superficialities had been cleared out of the way and it is always more difficult to engage in a frank exchange. But real things had begun to happen in terms of relationships between individuals. There was open disagreement and it is not easy to gain the freedom which permits this. The fact that it was possible for people to disagree yesterday without alienating one another was an indication of the value of the groups to you. These exchanges between professions and between people in different areas of their chosen vocation are of enormous value.

When I went into one group yesterday I saw the words "reach out" on the blackboard. It seems to me that we need to introduce into our lives the "reach-out" as opposed to the "teach-in" or the "sit-in." We are here reaching out for a mutual exchange between ourselves as professionals and individuals and with our children and young people.

Revue et commentaire: II

EN ASSISTANT À vos délibérations, on ne pouvait manquer de se rendre compte qu'en discutant des enfants, vous discutiez du monde entier. A une extrémité, on estimait que le soin des enfants est la responsabilité de la société tout entière ; à l'autre, que cette responsabilité pouvait être déléguée aux spécialistes. Le problème de savoir si on a vraiment le choix, et savoir comment choisir, les implications qui s'ensuivent, préoccupent un grand nombre d'entre vous. Vos discussions d'hier et mes commentaires peuvent se ramener aux grandes catégories établies par le Dr Rabinovitch dans son exposé.

Dans le domaine des valeurs, certains de vos groupes se préoccupent de la nature de la société et de sa responsabilité, directe ou par délégation, à l'égard du soin des enfants. C'est dans ce contexte que vous avez discuté l'automation, les loisirs, la pauvreté, tous les grands problèmes sociaux qui affectent enfants et adultes. On peut voir que certains d'entre vous ont écouté les jeunes et se sont rendu compte qu'ils apprennent à faire face à ces problèmes plus vite et avec plus d'agilité que nous. Quelques-uns parmi vous ont réfléchi à ce que les jeunes nous disent, et sur le moyen de s'organiser dans une société où tant de choix s'offrent et où la jeunesse jouit d'une liberté que nous n'avons jamais connue. On a longuement discuté avec intérêt de la nature, des buts et du succès de l' « Operation Headstart », aux Etats-Unis.

En parlant de quelques-uns des groupes professionnels auxquels nous avons délégué certaines responsabilités, le Dr Rabinovitch a créé chez beaucoup un certain souci. En nous occupant de professionnalisme, nous nous occupons du savoir et du pouvoir au sein de notre société. Certains groupes ont eu du mal à déterminer ce qui constitue un « professionnel ». S'agit-il simplement d'être extrêmement compétent dans sa propre sphère, ou bien y a-t-il d'autres responsabilités ? d'autres privilèges ? Voilà qui me semble un sujet de discussions riche en possibilités, car il soulève encore une fois le problème de la délégation des responsabilités, du réalisme de cette attitude, et de nos responsabilités, en tant que société, vis-à-vis de la formation et du comportement professionnels. Ce qui a peut-être été le plus utile, dans cette discussion, c'est la fréquence avec laquelle les groupes se sont penchés sur le bénévolat et sur les rapports entre professionnels et bénévoles.

Ceci a amené plusieurs groupes à passer au manque de temps pour former et contrôler le bénévole dont souffrent la plupart des professionnels, et à demander qu'on redéfinisse le rôle du professionnel et la responsabilité qu'il doit assumer pour permettre à de plus en plus de gens d'assumer certaines fonctions dans sa spécialité. A mon avis, c'est là une discussion très utile car, aujourd'hui, le besoin de plus de talent, d'intelligence, a augmenté dramatiquement ; donc il nous faut examiner de nouveau ce que l'on entend par « professionnel » et par le rôle d'un tel envers la société.

Vos discussions, souvent centrées sur les écoles, sont restées ambivalentes, sans déterminer si, d'un côté, l'école pouvait accomplir de façon satisfaisante tout ce qu'on attend d'elle ou, de l'autre côté, si on ne pouvait lui demander encore bien davantage. Il y a eu quelques discussions très ouvertes, et on peut sentir la possibilité de ces rapports entre professionnels que nous avons reconnus comme un de nos plus pressants problèmes.

De nombreux groupes se sont débattus avec le difficile problème, posé par le Dr Rabinovitch, de l'emploi de la force, et de l'obligation. On est tombé d'accord sur le fait que les domaines où s'exerce la liberté changent dans toutes les sociétés, et que nous devrons peut-être accepter une moins grande liberté de choix dans certains domaines, dans l'avenir.

Dans beaucoup de groupes, on pu constater des réactions variées et violentes devant les commentaires du Dr Rabinovitch sur la famille, vache sacrée. Certains pensent que la famille se porte bien, qu'il n'y a qu'à l'aider et à lui donner plus de force. D'autres estiment que la fonction de la famille évolue, et qu'il nous faut pouvoir faire face à l'idée de changement sans abandonner l'institution dans son essence. Il y a eu un certain malaise, dans plusieurs groupes, au sujet de l'intervention de la force ; on craint de voir s'affaiblir l'intégrité de la famille.

Tout au cours de la discussion sur la famille, on a pu voir se poser la question : comment établir le contact avec la famille ? Où la société atteint-elle la famille ? Combien de secteurs où se passe le contact pouvons-nous identifier ? Quels sont ceux qui ont lieu avant un échec ? Y en a-t-il qui puissent être préventifs plutôt que thérapeutiques ?

Il me semble que l'intervention forcée demande une discussion très nuancée. Par exemple, l'idée de l'éducation à la vie familiale obligatoire a soulevé un grand intérêt, mais la discussion semblait impliquer que nous, les spécialistes, pourrions dire aux familles comment agir. Vue sous l'angle de ma propre profession, cette idée m'amène à vous suggérer que, du point de vue éducation des adultes, c'est rempli de danger et que si nous voulons réussir, il faut arriver à un enseignement mutuel.

En ce qui concerne les réunions d'hier, il me semble que la plupart d'entre vous ont trouvé les discussions plus difficiles. Peut-être fallait-il s'y attendre, une fois le superficiel dépassé, il est des sujets toujours difficiles à aborder dans une discussion ouverte. Mais les rapports entre individus ont progressé. Le fait que l'on peut différer sans acrimonie indique bien la valeur qu'ont ces groupes pour vous. Ces échanges sont très importants pour les professions comme pour les individus, dans les divers secteurs des domaines qu'ils ont choisis.

En rendant visite à un groupe, hier, j'ai vu, au tableau noir, ces mots « Tendons la main ». Voilà, me semble-t-il, l'idée qu'il faut mettre dans notre vie à la place de l'inertie. Nous sommes ici pour tendre la main, pour parvenir à un échange entre nous, en tant que professionnels et en tant qu'individus, et entre nous et nos enfants et nos jeunes.

Roads to Maturity: Finding New Approaches

PROFESSOR CHARLES E. HENDRY

LAST AUGUST I had the privilege of being a member of a small programme team for a Canadian Assembly of Youth, at the University of Saskatchewan. Assembly '65, as it was called, was convened jointly by the Anglican Church of Canada and the United Church of Canada. It brought together almost as many young Canadians from coast to coast as we have adults in this Canadian Conference on Children. The concerns that brought us together for a week in Saskatoon were essentially identical with those that have brought us this week to Montréal.

One vivid memory I shall cherish always is the poignancy and tenderness of the folksongs that were a feature of the opening plenary sessions. We had Jerry Gray, of the Travellers, with us and he was always on hand with his guitar. Here was unmistakable, unobstructed communication; communication in an idiom that had meaning and validity, constituting, so it seemed to me, a new hymnology in the making, an hymnology in the tradition of the prophets, one of profound social protest and one of deepest yearning, but without, for the time being at least, the piety of the psalmist. Speaking of "Roads to Maturity," I am sure many of you are familiar with one of their favourite songs, one by Bob Dylan. It seems especially relevant.

> How many roads must a man walk down
> Before he becomes a man?
> The answer, my friend,
> The answer is blown in the wind.

The meaning to me seems clear. Youth is not looking for answers from us—from the church, from university professors, or from other adults who represent authority. For it, symbolically and significantly, the answers are "blown in the wind."

The poignancy of the situation is eloquently portrayed in the

Canadian film classic, *Nobody Waved Goodbye*. It was underlined for me several times during the Assembly, when, quite spontaneously, the whole group began singing that other Dylan song, "I can't help but wonder where I'm bound." In lighter vein, I am reminded of a young chap on a beach in Florida a year ago. He had been lying in the sun. He passed me as he left the beach and on the back of his sweat shirt I read these words: "Don't follow me: I don't know where I'm going."

I get the distinct impression that young people today, and especially university students, are intent upon substituting responsibility for respectability. George Grant's *Lament for a Nation* notwithstanding, they are more interested in manifest dignity than in manifest destiny. Chronic contempt is giving way to critical concern. At the very core of current dissent and protest, whether at Berkeley or Toronto, in Washington or Ottawa, over Vietnam, civil rights, or any other major issue of social policy, there is deep purpose, genuine commitment, unflinching courage, and sincere faith on the part of many. The nihilists and anarchists of course are still active. Communists also are as busy as ever, fanning the flames of disenchantment and disillusionment. What comes through clearly, however, when one reads the more discerning and disciplined accounts of the Berkeley disturbance is that youth is not interested in abstract ideologies or particular political parties. It is fed up with dogma, whether economic, political, or social, and with pervasive pettiness, waste, and pretense.

Youth may seem far out, but deep down it is in revolt: in revolt against the very meaning of meaninglessness. It is anti-wasteland, anti-alienation, utterly fed up with prevailing and uncritical assumptions of futility, determined to move up closer into the control rooms of destiny.

Young people now constitute what might be called, with apologies to Pierre Berton, "The Uncomfortable Few," but what is really important is that they are becoming uncomfortable about being uncomfortable. What we are witnessing in our very midst—and this despite the deplorable excesses of misguided extremists—to the accompaniment of jazz in cellar clubs, poetry in coffee houses, and folksongs in cluttered college retreats—is not a breakdown in the morals of youth, but a breakthrough in morale.

A few years ago I was obliged to spend several weeks in hospital. One morning as I lay in my bed, my attention became focused on a solitary fly on the window of my room. The fly was located on an upper pane of glass. The window itself was slightly raised at the bottom edge. At first, as if by deliberation, the fly moved time and time again around the periphery of the section to which it had become attached. Then it would crawl diagonally, or so it seemed, until in desperation it would take off in a mad fury, returning only to crash against the deceptive transparency. Its frantic reconnaissance began afresh as it moved monotonously back and forth horizontally across the full surface of the window's pane. Random movements followed, punctuated again by furious flight, ending always in near disaster. For whole minutes, as if stunned into stupor, the fly would remain motionless. Energy restored, it would commence its futile gyrations again, alternating crawl and crash, sometimes slowly, jerkily, and with hesitation, more often like a firecracker, out of control, careening crazily around the ceiling. In utter fascination, my eyes followed this fly for almost an hour. It had me mesmerized. At last, exhausted by this strange exercise, I fell asleep, not, however, before I had recorded a passing commentary in my mind.

This fly, I said to myself, is a prisoner of his frame of reference, or more probably, of his lack of a frame of reference. If flight into freedom was its object, if indeed any objective existed at all, then there was an obvious avenue of escape. An adequate passage was readily accessible at the bottom of the window. Driven by instinct alone, bereft of reason, caught up in meaningless space, behaviour could only be blind, and it could end only in frustration, fury, and futility. Without suggesting specific application, the allegorical reference of this episode must be readily apparent.

In my humble view, you and I are caught in the limitations of our frame of reference. T. S. Eliot may have had this in mind when he asked

> Where is the life we have lost in living?
> Where is the wisdom we have lost in knowledge?

We, too, need a breakthrough in morale: that is to say, it is imperative that we achieve clarity as to our objectives—what we are for, not just what we're against; conviction as to their importance and some ordering of priorities among them; confidence in our capacity as individuals, as professionals, and as representatives of agencies, organizations, and institutions, that we can achieve such objectives.

I commend to you two instructive, provocative, and inspiring books that have helped me immensely these last few weeks in clearing my mental decks for action. I refer to Michael Harrington's new book, *The Accidental Century* and Harvey Cox's *The Secular City* (both Macmillan publications of current vintage). In urging that you give serious attention to these two volumes, I am frank to admit a certain identification with the clown in the parable which Harvey Cox borrows from the writings of Kierkegaard, which I now quote:

A travelling circus once broke into flames just after it had encamped outside a Danish village. The manager turned to the performers who were already dressed for their acts and sent the clown to call the villagers to help put out the fire, which could not only destroy the circus but might race through the dry fields and envelope the town itself. Dashing pell-mell to the village square, the painted clown shouted to everyone to come to the circus and help put out the fire. The villagers laughed and applauded this novel way of tricking them into coming to the big top. The clown wept and pleaded. He insisted that he was not putting on an act but the town really was in mortal danger. The more he implored the more the villagers howled . . . until the fire leaped across the fields and spread to the town itself. Before the villagers knew it, their homes had been destroyed.

Those of you who have seen *Camelot* will remember that delightful episode when, in utter exasperation, King Pellinore turned to King Arthur and said, "Arthur, you've got to stop thinking thoughts and think something." Possibly you may be equally impatient with me. In any case, let us now seek to follow Bergson's dictum and try "to think as men of action and then act as men of thought."

Much that I will attempt to suggest by way of "approaches to action" has been implicit in what Dr. Alan Ross and Dr. Sam Rabinovitch have said already and in the wise commentary by Dr. Alan Thomas. My task and your task, this morning and this afternoon, is to identify some of these ideas, sort them out carefully, and translate them into explicit and concrete proposals for action. Whether they be narrow paths, winding paths, highways, or expressways, we want "to get where the action is" and be on our way.

I leave it to you to determine which tasks and sets of problems require what Alan Thomas has termed "technical solutions" and which "moral solutions." Most of them, I suspect, will require a combination of competence and compassion. I propose that we focus our attention and mobilize our utmost creative effort around six major tasks.

First, let us tackle the problem of communication. I suggest, as a basic premise, that we stop talking about why and how we should or might collaborate and simply begin collaborating. I suggest that instead of engaging in polite and formal dialogue, we deploy ourselves in certain joint undertakings. I suggest, without prejudice to any other group, that we begin by ensuring that, in every such collaborative initiative, representatives from health, education, and welfare (broadly interpreted) be included.

May I give an illustration. This will be the fourth consecutive year that we, at the University of Toronto, will have convened an interprofessional student-faculty seminar. Graduating students and senior faculty representatives from as many as ten different professional faculties, schools, and institutes come together for one full day, to confront some one common problem together. The first year we began the seminar with four cases of neglect and abuse of children. The cases were presented within the first hour by a pediatrician, a psychiatrist, a psychologist, and a social worker. The first case, the one presented by the pediatrician, was illustrated by coloured slides. Even the most experienced among us that morning will not soon forget that first slide. It showed an infant's head from which a large hole had been chewed by a rat. The social history indicated that this had occurred while the child lay in bed between two inebriated adults in a slum area of downtown Toronto.

In the small interprofessional discussion groups that followed that general session, and in the closing session that afternoon, something very vital and meaningful happened, so vital and so valuable that this Interprofessional Student-Faculty one-day seminar has become an established and respected continuing exercise in interprofessional collaboration on our campus.

Because we were confronted initially by actual cases rather than by abstract ideas genuine communication was achieved. In the process, difficulties with language and specialized, professional terminology were dealt with on the spot. Acceptance of and respect for precision of meaning replaced irritation and intolerance because understanding was essential if one was to keep one's eye on the ball—the child and his condition. As Alfred North Whitehead has remarked, with penetrating insight, "The process is the actuality."

This, I suspect, is what Alan Thomas had in mind when he suggested that when the need arises to redefine a situation in fairly fundamental terms, the opportunity also arises for social inventiveness. If this be so, let us hope that professional leaders, in the fields of health, education, and welfare, will seize upon situations that urgently require such basic redefinition. Exciting and exacting exercises in interprofessional collaboration await us on every hand as we move in to pioneer new frontiers of human service. And may I remind all of us that, in all probability, the greatest unexplored frontier ahead is time itself, time released by the cybernetic revolution and the resulting massive expansion of non-work.

In the second place let us turn to the discovery, development, and deployment of professional personnel. At the very outset, may I plead for some over-all policy and strategy that embraces all of the relevant professions in health, education, and welfare. Surely we can approach the task of interpretation, recruiting, and selection co-operatively, with solid, built-in, mutual reinforcements. We simply cannot afford the luxury and license of competition in this area. And what about the curricula of our professional schools? Two points have been made repeatedly during this Conference that have important implications here. We all agree, I believe, that each of the human service professions needs substantial and systematic underpinning in the behavioural sciences, in human growth and the social environment, and in the dynamics of planned social change. How can we assist one another in providing such foundation courses? We agree, too, I believe, that each of our professions needs basic education and intensive training in the understanding and disciplined practice of sensitivity, of relationship, of listening, and of liberating the human spirit. How can we learn from one another in this area?

We have our teaching hospitals in the medical schools, our practice teaching schools in education, and our field instruction centres in social work. How can we enrich such teaching centres in the interest of greater effectiveness in ultimate interprofessional teamwork after graduation? Would there be value in establishing regional teaching laboratories for the joint use of the relevant professional schools by using camps in the summer—camps for the physically handicapped or mentally retarded children, camps for diabetic children, and camps for normal, run-of-the-mill children? The very isolation of the camp setting and the continuous day-long, week to week, or month to month contact between the student professionals and the children offers unusual advantages for professional education.

Is it unrealistic to hope that some of the new professional schools being created or shortly to be created in some of our universities—for example, the new Faculty of Medicine being projected for McMaster University—might not be encouraged deliberately to experiment with an enriched interprofessional component in their programmes?

Is it fanciful to hope that one day provision will be made to bring recent graduates from a variety of different professional schools back, say after five years in practice in the field, for an intensive refresher course, complete with feed back and the fullest possible interchange on an interprofessional basis?

Thirdly, what about the place of the indigenous non-professional and the volunteer? Someone has written, recently, that "Dollar amounts can serve to express the value of a material service, but, in social welfare terms (that is, in terms of well-being), the significant measure is time, time given and time received out of one human life to help another human being. This is the ultimate scarcity in social economics."

There is massive evidence available, which I have no need to cite, that the age of automation is upon us. Time, especially time released from the demands of the production of material goods, the management of such production, and even the distribution of the finished product, is soon going to be available in overwhelming abundance. The leisure class is being transformed before our very eyes into the leisure mass. We have scarcely begun to speculate upon, let alone design, social and public policy with this momentous new resource in mind.

Ingenious use is now being made of what are being called "indigenous non-professionals." Human service careers for the poor, for married women, for older people, and for teen-aged youth are being developed particularly across the border, on a vast scale. These efforts have passed the dry-run, demonstration stage. In my view, with a few notable exceptions such as the Junior League, we have been irresponsibly unimaginative in our approach to the mobilization of non-professionals and volunteers. Let us not forget what Sam Rabinovitch said to us. He envisions a model of work, time, and leisure in which an individual will have two jobs, a work-centred and a service-centred job. Combining this notion with the fact that most of today's teenagers will probably change their occupations several times in their lifetime, we face not only the inevitability of continuous education, but also the problem of entry and re-entry into "occupational space." We must conquer social space as well as outer space.

In the fourth place we turn our attention to organizational structure and institutional arrangements. Students of general systems theory and its relationships and implications for organization and administration have a great deal to say to us on this score. One of the most concise and cogent contributions is now available in a volume published by the University of Toronto Press under the title *Welfare and Wisdom*. This volume contains lectures given in celebration of the Fiftieth Anniversary of our School of Social Work in Toronto. The two lectures which were given by Dr. Eugene Pusić of the University of Zagreb are particularly relevant. The burden of his brilliant exposition favours substitution of task- or problem-oriented organizational units for traditional hierarchical structures.

To cope effectively with steadily expanding and increasingly more and more complex service programmes, particularly where interprofessional and interdisciplinary co-operation is involved and where interagency and interprovincial collaboration is required, new organizational and administrative arrangements must be developed. Computer technology must be placed at the disposal of management. If illustrations are needed of how new forms must be fashioned to fit new functions, one might site the task force that has been created in the office of the Prime Minister in Ottawa to mount the war on poverty in Canada. Another illustration is an interdivisional committee within the Canadian Welfare Council, involving Child and Family Welfare, Public Welfare, and Corrections, which is to draft a policy statement with respect to planned parenthood. We are familiar, also, I believe, with the Central Registry that has been created in British Columbia, which provides essential data on children in receipt of some form of care—medical, educational, psychological, social—and which makes such information available for appropriate professional use.

Fifthly, I simply propose to identify a few areas, actually three in number, in which bold, strategic thrusts are overdue. I would put prevention first in this brief inventory. We insist that we are utterly distressed with the job so many of us are doing, namely, the job of patching up. Public health is held up as a model and so it is and for its magnificent achievements, we salute it. We must do more than salute it, however; we must find ways, in education and particularly in welfare, to emulate public health. I can report, happily, that a group of senior public welfare executives from all over Canada met last August in Fredericton for this very purpose. I am confident that, when the proceedings of those work sessions are available, we will see some very encouraging results.

We face great difficulties in the applied social sciences. A year ago I was asked to appear before the Standing Committee on External Affairs to testify on the question of hate literature. One paragraph from that testimony I would like to read into the record:

> Hate pollutes the mind of man in much the same way that Strontium 90 pollutes the water and the milk he drinks, sulphur dioxide fouls the air he breathes, and lead and arsenic, on occasion, poison the food he eats. Unfortunately, however, there is a difference. Public health officials can measure tolerance levels of pollution with scientific precision. In the case of air and food they do so in terms of parts per million, in the case of water in microcuries per litre, in the case of Strontium 90 in micromicrocuries per litre. And public opinion, attuned to the authority of science, in consequence, supports control (however effectively implemented) through formal legislation.

This paragraph is quoted by way of transition to a second area where special thrust is needed: research. Here again, in comparison with public health, education and social welfare continue to be at a distinct disadvantage. It is only within the past few years, notably with the creation of the Welfare Grants Administration in the Department of National Health and Welfare and with the creation of A.R.D.A. (the Agricultural Rehabilitation and Development Administration) and some of our royal commissions that substantial funds have been made available for research that is focused on social functioning and dysfunctioning. I very much wish I had brought with me the set of maps of "Social and Economic Disadvantage" produced by A.R.D.A., showing the incidence of infant mortality, applications for employment, levels of education, average family incomes, etc. for every census tract, county, and province in Canada. We should paste those on our walls and look at them every day. They are magnificent.

I am pleased also to report that it is the intention of the Ontario Department of Public Welfare, when the new Child Welfare Act comes into effect in January 1966, to undertake a longitudinal research project that will follow a sample of "children in care" throughout the entire province over a period of twenty-five years.

Dr. Alan Ross spoke of the need in the practice of medicine for what he called "radical surgery." Dr. Sam Rabinovitch suggested the existence of something that might be called "social malignancy." They each urged that a joint effort be made, experimentally, to deal with the "battered child" and with "the chronic hard-core, multi-problem family." Why not? Why not examine what is now being done in various cities across Canada and see what more can be done, and then make sure that it is done?

My final reference is to the approach of "community development." Whether one thinks of a local project such as Ed Smee is heading in Lanark County in Ontario, the pioneer efforts among the Indian population of Manitoba, or the massive A.R.D.A.-B.A.E.Q. project in the Gaspé in the Province of Quebec, here is a kind of social invention that has tremendous possibilities. I myself am intensely interested in it and next month will be taking off for seven months to find out what I can learn about it in Mexico, Peru, and Puerto Rico, and I hope to record my findings and make them available for use here back home. I am convinced that we in this so-called relatively highly developed country have a great deal to learn as we approach our under-developed areas from the so-called relatively under-developed countries.

Sixthly, how about this conference itself, our Canadian Conference on Children? I am purposely leaving this as a question. Specific proposals have been drafted for your consideration in provincial committees tonight and for general discussion on Thursday.

In closing, may I suggest that we refer back to Dr. Alva Myrdal's address Sunday evening and to Dr. Alan Thomas' perceptive observations Tuesday morning, that competence is not enough if we are to achieve the objectives we have in mind. Concern, compassion, and commitment are even more basic. What Dr. Alan Gregg of the Rockefeller Foundation said about medicine applies equally to every other service profession: "The mistakes that have been made in medicine have not been made by men who don't know, but by men who don't care."

Les chemins de la maturité: quelques nouvelles méthodes

AU MOIS D'AOÛT DERNIER, j'ai eu le privilège de faire partie d'une équipe de travail de la Canadian Assembly of Youth, à l'University of Saskatchewan. « Assembly '65 », comme on l'appelait, a eu lieu sous les auspices combinées de l'Anglican Church et de la United Church of Canada. Elle a réuni presque autant de jeunes Canadiens, de toutes les régions du pays, qu'il y a aujourd'hui d'adultes présents à ce congrès. Les préoccupations qui nous ont réunis durant une semaine à Saskatoon étaient, essentiellement, identiques à celles qui nous rassemblent cette semaine à Montréal.

Il est un souvenir que je garderai toujours précieusement en mémoire... c'est le son, à la fois poignant et tendre, des chansons folkloriques qui ont marqué la séance plénière d'ouverture. Il y avait là Jerry Gray, du groupe des « Travellers », toujours prêt à prendre sa guitare. Et entre nous il existait, réel et profond, un sentiment de participation, de communication, de communication dans une langue ayant à la fois sens et validité. Ces chants me semblaient de nouveaux psaumes, écrits dans la vraie tradition des prophètes, une tradition de protestations sociales et de profonde nostalgie, mais privés, temporairement du moins, de la piété du psalmiste.

En parlant des « Chemins de la maturité », je suis sûr que bon nombre d'entre vous connaissent une des chansons favorites de ces jeunes, une chanson de Bob Dylan. Elle semble particulièrement significative :

> How many roads must a man walk down
> Before he becomes a man?
> The answer, my friend,
> The answer is blown in the wind.*

Le sens de tout cela me paraît assez clair. Les jeunes ne se tournent plus vers nous pour trouver les réponses à leurs questions. Pour eux, la réponse, c'est le vent qui l'apporte.

Un film canadien, devenu un classique, dépeint bien le poignant de la situation. Il s'agit de « Nobody waved Good-bye ». Je m'en suis rendu compte mieux que jamais au cours de cette « Assembly », quand spontanément le groupe tout entier se mit à chanter l'autre chanson de Bob Dylan « I can't help but wonder where I'm bound »†.

Et, dans un contexte moins sérieux, je pense à ce garçon qui l'an dernier était étendu sur une plage de Florida. En s'en allant, il est passé auprès de moi et j'ai pu lire, sur sa chemise « Ne me suivez pas, je ne sais pas où je vais ».

J'ai l'impression très nette que la jeunesse d'aujourd'hui, et surtout la jeunesse universitaire, s'est décidée à remplacer respectabilité par responsabilité. Quoi qu'en dise George Grant dans son *Lament for a Nation*, la dignité leur semble plus importante que la destinée. Le mépris chronique est remplacé petit à petit par une préoccupation critique. Au cœur même des désagréments et des protestations actuelles, que ce soit à Toronto ou à Berkeley, à Washington ou à Ottawa, qu'il s'agisse du Viet Nam ou des droits civiques, ou de n'importe quel grave problème social, il y a un sentiment profond d'engagement, un courage qui ne se dément pas et une foi sincère chez la plupart. Bien sûr, anarchistes et nihilistes n'ont pas désarmé. Et les communistes non plus ne restent pas inactifs, cherchant toujours à raviver la flamme du désenchantement et des désillusions. Ce qui apparaît clairement, toutefois, lorsqu'on lit les compte rendus plus sérieux et plus approfondis de troubles comme ceux qui ont eu lieu à Berkeley, c'est que la jeunesse ne s'intéresse pas aux idéologies abstraites ou aux partis politiques en

*Combien de chemins doit parcourir un homme / Avant d'être vraiment homme ? / La réponse, ami, c'est le vent qui l'apporte.

† « Comment ne pas me demander où je vais ».

particulier. Ils en ont assez des dogmes, qu'ils soient économiques, politiques ou sociaux ; ils en ont assez de la mesquinerie, du gaspillage et des affectations. La jeunesse peut sembler déséquilibrée. En réalité, elle se révolte, elle se révolte contre le sens même du non-sens. Elle ne veut plus du vide, de l'aliénation ; elle en a assez ; elle ne veut plus de cette futilité qu'on lui impute sans réserve. Elle veut prendre les commandes de son propre destin.

La jeunesse d'aujourd'hui est une jeunesse inconfortable, et son inconfort présent naît de ce qu'elle se sent inconfortable. Ce qui se passe sous nos yeux, et malgré les excès malheureux de quelques extrémistes mal guidés, au son des guitares dans les caves, au rythme des vers dans les cafés ou des chants de folklore dans les chambres de collège, ce n'est pas un abaissement de la morale chez les jeunes, c'est une revitalisation du moral.

Il y a quelques années, j'ai dû passer plusieurs semaines à l'hôpital. Un matin, alors que j'étais couché, le manège d'une mouche sur la fenètre de ma chambre attira mon attention. La mouche se promenait sur le carreau supérieur. La vitre était entrouverte au bas. Au début, comme si elle le faisait exprès, la mouche a fait je ne sais combien de fois le tour du carreau sur lequel elle était. Ensuite elle l'a abordé en diagonale. Enfin en désespoir de cause, elle s'est envolée pour se heurter durement à la transparence trompeuse de la vitre. Son manège affolé a alors recommencé. En avant, en arrière, en travers. Puis l'envol furieux suivi de l'écrasement brutal. Pendant plusieurs minutes, comme assommée, la mouche restait immobile. Puis, son énergie retrouvée, elle recommençait son futile tourbillon évoluant comme un ressort sans contrôle. Totalement fasciné, j'ai suivi des yeux cette mouche pendant près d'une heure ; elle m'hypnotisait. A la fin, littéralement épuisé, je me suis endormi, non sans qu'un parallèle ne s'établisse dans mon esprit.

Cette mouche, me suis-je dit, est prisonnière de son système de coordonnées ou plutôt de son manque de système de coordonnées. Si l'envol vers la liberté était son but, si en fait elle avait un but, il y avait un chemin qui lui permettait visiblement de s'évader. Au bas de la fenêtre, il y avait un passage dont elle aurait pu se servir. N'étant conduite que par l'instinct, sans raison, au cœur d'un espace pour elle désorienté, elle ne pouvait agir qu'en aveugle et son comportement ne pouvait résulter qu'en frustration, fureur et futilité. Sans vouloir suggérer d'application précise, il me semble qu'il est facile de transposer ce curieux épisode.

A mon humble avis, vous et moi sommes prisonniers de notre système de coordonnées. C'est peut-être ce à quoi songeait T. S. Eliot quand il écrivait*

> Where is the life we have lost in living?
> Where is the wisdom we have lost in knowledge?

Nous aussi, nous avons besoin de revitaliser notre moral. Il faut, autrement dit, que nous envisagions avec clarté nos buts : ce que nous voulons, ce à quoi nous nous opposons. Il faut la conviction de leur importance et de leur ordre d'importance ; et enfin il faut que nous ayons confiance dans nos capacités en tant qu'individus, en tant que professionnels, en tant que représentants d'agences, d'organisations et d'institutions, et l'assurance que nous pouvons atteindre ces buts.

Je vous recommande la lecture de deux livres intéressants, qui font réfléchir et qui encouragent à la fois, et qui m'ont beaucoup aidé, au cours des dernières semaines, à me préparer à l'action. D'abord le nouveau livre de Michael Harrington, *The Accidental Century*, ensuite celui de Harvey Cox, *The Secular City*, tous deux publiés chez Macmillan. En vous demandant de lire et d'approfondir ces deux livres, j'admets bien franchement que je ressens un certain sentiment d'identité avec le clown de la parabole de Kierkegaard, cité par Harvey Cox. Voici ce que dit Kierkegaard :

> Il advint qu'un incendie éclata dans un cirque ambulant qui venait de s'installer à la lisière d'un village danois. Le directeur appela tous les artistes, déjà maquillés et habillés, et envoya le clown chercher les villageois afin qu'ils aident à maîtriser l'incendie qui menaçait non seulement tout le cirque mais aussi les champs et le village lui-même. Courant par la grand place de village, le clown cria de son mieux à l'aide et pria les villageois de venir combattre l'incendie. Les villageois rirent et applaudirent, pensant que c'était là le numéro du clown. Et plus il pleurait et suppliait, et plus ils riaient... jusqu'au moment où les flammes enveloppèrent le village. Avant même que les villageois ne s'en soient rendu compte, le village n'existait plus.

Ceux qui, parmi vous, ont vu *Camelot* se souviendront de ce charmant épisode au cours duquel, excédé, le roi Pellinore se tourne vers le roi Arthur et lui dit : « Arthur, il est temps que tu t'arrêtes de penser à des pensées, et que tu te mettes à penser à quelque chose ». Peut-être éprouvez-vous la même impatience à mon égard. De toute façon, essayons de suivre Bergson quand il nous recommande de « penser comme des hommes d'action et d'agir comme des hommes qui pensent ».

*Où est la vie que nous avons perdue tant que nous vivions ? / Où est la sagesse que nous avons perdue dans tout notre savoir ?

Une grande partie de ce que je veux suggérer en fait de méthodes pour passer à l'action est implicite dans ce que le Dr Alan Ross et le Dr Sam Rabinovitch vous ont déjà dit, ainsi que dans le profond et spirituel commentaire du Dr Alan Thomas. Ma tâche et la vôtre, au cours de cette journée, c'est d'identifier quelques-unes de ces idées, de les faire ressortir soigneusement, et de les traduire en termes d'action possible de façon explicite et concrète. Que ce soient des sentiers étroits, ou tortueux, des grandes routes ou des voies rapides qui nous amènent à l'action, nous voulons y parvenir et commencer dès maintenant.

Je vous laisse le soin de déterminer quelles sont les tâches et les problèmes qui requièrent des solutions techniques et ceux qui requièrent des solutions morales, selon la distinction faite par le Dr Thomas. La plupart demandent, me semble-t-il, un mélange de compétence et de compassion. Je vous propose maintenant de concentrer notre attention et de nous consacrer à six tâches des plus importantes.

D'abord, occupons-nous du problème de communication. Je suggère, pour commencer, que nous cessions de discuter pourquoi et comment nous devrions collaborer, et de commencer, tout simplement, à collaborer. Je suggère qu'au lieu d'entamer des dialogues polis et pleins de formalité, nous commencions d'entreprendre ensemble certaines tâches communes. Je suggère que, sans préjugé vis-à-vis d'aucun autre groupe, nous commencions par nous assurer que dans toute initiative conjointe de ce genre soient inclus des représentants des domaines de la santé, de l'éducation et du bien-être, pris au sens le plus large.

Puis-je vous donner un exemple? Pour la quatrième année consécutive, à l'University of Toronto, nous allons organiser une rencontre interprofessionnelle des étudiants et du corps professoral. Des étudiants de dernière année et des représentants du corps professoral d'au moins dix facultés, écoles et instituts vont se réunir pendant une journée afin d'étudier ensemble un problème commun important. La première année, nous avons commencé cette rencontre avec quatre cas d'enfants négligés et maltraités. Les cas ont été présentés au cours de la première heure par un pédiatre, un psychiatre, un psychologue et un travailleur social. Le premier cas, présenté par un pédiatre, était accompagné de diapositives en couleurs. Même les plus endurcis parmi nous ne pourront jamais oublier cette première diapositive : la tête d'un enfant et le trou béant qu'y avait fait la morsure d'un rat. Cela s'était produit alors que l'enfant était couché entre deux adultes ivres, dans un taudis de Toronto.

Au cours des discussions par petits groupes qui ont suivi cette réunion générale, au cours de la séance de clôture qui eut lieu dans l'après-midi, il s'est passé quelque chose de très important et de très significatif. Tellement important que cette rencontre interprofessionnelle d'une journée est devenue un des exercices en collaboration « interdisciplines » les plus estimés et les plus appréciés de notre université.

En abordant des cas réels au lieu de discuter de généralités abstraites, on a pu arriver à une communication réelle. Il a été possible de surmonter les problèmes de langage spécialisé et de terminologie, sur place. L'acceptation et le respect de la précision des termes a remplacé l'irritation et l'intolérance, parce qu'il était essentiel de bien se comprendre si l'on voulait s'en ternir à l'essentiel, c'est à dire à l'enfant et à son milieu. Comme l'a remarqué avec clairvoyance Alfred North Whitehead, « Le procédé, c'est la réalité ».

Je pense que c'est ce que voulait dire Alan Thomas en suggérant que, lorsqu'il devient nécessaire de redéfinir une situation en termes fondamentaux, on a ainsi l'occasion de faire preuve de créativité sociale. S'il en est ainsi, espérons que les responsables professionnels dans les domaines de la santé, de l'éducation et du bien-être, s'empareront de cas où la re-définition est essentielle. De passionnants et difficiles exercices en collaboration interprofessionnelle nous attendent partout où nous voudrons avancer dans le domaine des services humains. Et puis-je me permettre de vous rappeler que la frontière la plus vaste, et la moins explorée, c'est en réalité le temps, le temps conçu en termes de la révolution cybernétique et de l'expansion massive du « non-travail » qui en résulte.

En second, parlons de la découverte, de la formation et du déploiement du personnel professionnel. Au tout début, puis-je demander instamment qu'il y ait une ligne de conduite générale concernant le personnel dans les professions qui ressortent de la santé, de l'éducation et du bien-être. Sûrement il doit être possible de faire face à la tâche d'interpréter, de recruter et de sélectionner en collaboration, en nous soutenant mutuellement. Nous ne pouvons nous offrir le luxe de rivaliser dans ce domaine. Et que dire des programmes de formation qu'offrent nos écoles ? On a répété deux choses bien souvent au cours de ce congrès, deux choses qui ont des implications graves. Nous sommes tous d'accord, il me semble, pour admettre que chacune des professions humaines demande une base solide dans les sciences du comportement, de la croissance et du milieu social, ainsi que dans les dynamiques d'une évolution sociale dirigée. Comment pouvons-nous nous aider à donner ces cours essentiels ? Nous sommes aussi d'accord, je veux le croire, pour admettre que nos professions demandent toutes une éducation de base et une formation intensive dans la compréhension et la discipline de la sensibilité, des relations interpersonnelles ; il faut savoir écouter, libérer les esprits. Que pouvons-nous apprendre les uns des autres dans ce domaine ?

Nous avons, en médecine, des hopitaux universitaires ; l'éducation a ses écoles normales et le service social des centres de formation. Comment enrichir toutes ces écoles pour rendre plus efficace le travail d'équipe qui sera plus tard celui de leurs diplômés ? Serait-ce une bonne chose que d'établir des laboratoires d'enseignement régionaux pour les écoles qui en dépendent, pourrait-on se servir des camps d'été pour jeunes handicapés, pour débiles mentaux, pour diabétiques, pour enfants normaux ? Le fait matériel de l'isolement du camp, et le contact quotidien avec les enfants durant plusieurs mois offrent des avantages spéciaux pour la formation professionnelle.

Serait-ce manquer de réalisme que d'espérer que quelques-unes des nouvelles grandes écoles (je pense entre autres à la Faculté de médecine qu'on envisage pour McMaster) soient encouragées à établir un programme interprofessionnel ? Est-ce rêver que d'espérer qu'un jour on pourra amener de nouveaux diplômés des diverses disciplines à revenir, disons après cinq ans de travail, dans le domaine de leur choix, pour suivre un cours de perfectionnement avec étude et partage de leurs expériences avec d'autres professionnels ?

Troisièmement, quelle place faire à l'individu non-professionnel, sur place, et au bénévole ? Quelqu'un a écrit récemment, que « les dollars peuvent traduire la valeur de services matériels, mais qu'en termes de bien-être social, il faut penser en termes de temps, temps donné, temps reçu, échange entre deux êtres humains, l'un aidant l'autre. Voilà le plus difficile et le plus rare, en économie sociale ».

Je n'ai pas besoin d'enumérer le tas des faits montrant que nous sommes à l'âge de l'automation. Le temps, le temps récupéré des exigences de la production des biens matériels, de la direction de cette production et même de la distribution du produit, sera bientôt plus qu'abondant. La classe oisive se transforme sous nos yeux en masse oisive. Nous avons à peine commencé d'envisager, et pas encore abordé, l'organisation sociale et publique de ces loisirs.

On se sert en ce moment, de façon ingénieuse, de ce qu'on appelle l'individu non-professionnel, sur place. Les carrières dans les services offerts aux indigents, aux femmes mariées, aux gens âgés, aux adolescents, s'organisent, surtout de l'autre côté de la frontière, sur une vaste échelle. Ces services ont maintenant dépassé le stade expérimental.

A mon avis, à part quelques remarquables exceptions comme la

Ligue de la jeunesse, nous avons totalement manqué d'imagination en essayant d'utiliser les services des bénévoles. Il ne faut pas oublier ce que nous a dit Sam Rabinovitch. Il envisage un modèle de travail et de loisirs dans lequel un individu aura deux occupations, une dans le monde du travail, une dans le monde du service. En ajoutant à cette idée le fait que la plupart des adolescents d'aujourd'hui devront changer de métier une ou plusieurs fois au cours de leur existence, nous faisons face à la nécessité inévitable de l'éducation sans cesse poursuivie et aussi au problème de l'entrée et du retour dans « l'espace professionnel ». Nous devons conquérir l'espace social tout comme l'espace proprement dit.

Quatrièmement, il nous faut accorder notre attention à la structure des organisations et à l'arrangement des institutions. Ceux qui ont étudié la théorie des systèmes généraux, ses rapports et ses implications dans l'organisation et l'administration, ont beaucoup à dire. Une des contributions les plus précises et les plus pertinentes à ce sujet a été publiée par University of Toronto Press dans un livre sous le titre *Welfare and Wisdom* ; c'est un recueil de conférences prononcées à l'occasion du cinquantenaire de notre Ecole de service social. Et parmi toutes ces conférences, celles – il y en a deux – prononcées par le Dr Eugène Pusić de l'université de Zagreb sont particulièrement intéressantes. Dans son brillant exposé, il se prononce en faveur de la substitution de cellules organisées, orientées vers un tâche ou un problème, à la structure hiérarchique traditionnelle.

Pour entreprendre efficacement des services de plus en plus nombreux et complexes, surtout lorsque la collaboration interprofessionnelle et interdisciplines entre en jeu, et quand il faut qu'agences et provinces coopèrent, il faut une nouvelle organisation administrative. Les techniques des ordinateurs électroniques doivent être mises à la disposition des dirigeants. Si l'on veut un exemple montrant comment il faut créer de nouveaux formats pour convenir à de nouvelles fonctions, on peut citer l'organisation créée dans les bureaux du premier ministre à Ottawa, pour entreprendre la bataille contre la pauvreté. Un autre exemple, c'est le comité multisections au sein du Conseil canadien du bien-être, où des responsables du bien-être de l'enfance et de la famille, du bien-être public et des services correctionnels ont collaboré pour établir une ligne de conduite concernant le contrôle des naissances. Nous sommes tout familiers, je crois, avec le système de registre central qui existe en Colombie britannique, qui fournit des renseignements sur les enfants qui reçoivent certains soins médicaux et qui bénéficient de services de rééducation, psychologiques et sociaux, registre qui met ces renseignements à la disposition des professionnels qui en ont besoin.

Cinquièmement, je veux identifier quelques secteurs, trois secteurs, en fait, dans lesquels il est plus que temps de passer à l'action. Je mettrai la prévention en tête de liste. Nous parlons tous du découragement que nous éprouvons en nous rendant compte du travail de retapage et de recollage que nous devons faire, et nous citons la Santé publique comme un modèle – et c'en est un, avec de magnifiques réussites à son actif – mais il ne suffit pas de s'incliner devant un paragon, il faut trouver le moyen, dans les domaines de l'éducation et du bien-être, d'en faire autant. Je suis heureux de dire qu'un groupe de dirigeants dans le domaine du bien-être, venant de toutes les régions du Canada, s'est réuni en août dernier à Fredericton dans ce but précis, et je suis sûr que, lorsque nous aurons les compte-rendus de ces séances, nous y trouverons des résultats encourageants.

Les sciences sociales appliquées posent des problèmes sérieux. Il y a un an, j'ai dû témoigner devant le Comité permanent des affaires étrangères, sur le problème de la propagande raciale. J'aimerais vous lire un paragraphe de mon témoignage :

> La haine pollue l'esprit de l'homme de la même façon que le Strontium 90 contamine l'eau et le lait qu'il boit, l'anhydride sulfureux corrompt l'air qu'il respire et parfois le plomb et l'arsénique empoisonnent ses aliments. Malheureusement, il y a une différence. Les autorités de la santé publique peuvent mesurer de façon précise le seuil de tolérance dans tous ces cas. Quand il s'agit du lait et des aliments, ils le font en parts par millions, pour l'eau il s'agit de microcuries par litre et pour le Strontium 90, de micromicrocuries par litre. Et l'opinion publique, qui respecte la science, soutient tout effort de réglementation, si insuffisant soit-il, par l'intermédiaire des lois.

Si je cite ce paragraphe, c'est en manière de transition pour aborder le second secteur où des mesures énergiques sont indispensables : celui de la recherche. Ici encore, en comparaison avec la santé publique, l'éducation et le bien-être sont très en retard. Ce n'est que depuis ces dernières années et surtout depuis la création du service de l'Administration des subventions au bien-être, au ministère de la Santé et du bien-être public, depuis la création de A.R.D.A. et l'établissement de certaines commissions royales que des fonds importants ont été consacrés aux recherches sur les problèmes sociaux.

J'aimerais avoir sous la main les tableaux mis au point par A.R.D.A. sur le sous-développement social et économique, donnant les incidences de mortalité infantile, les demandes d'emploi, le niveau d'éducation, les revenus familiaux moyens, dans toutes les régions du Canada. Nous devrions les accrocher au mur et les contempler chaque jour. Ils sont remarquables.

Je suis heureux de pouvoir dire que le ministère du bien-être public d'Ontario a l'intention, lorsque la nouvelle loi sur le bien-être social de l'enfance entrera en vigueur en janvier 1966, d'entreprendre une étude longitudinale sur un échantillonage d'enfants pris en charge dans toute la province sur une période de vingt-cinq ans.

Le Dr Alan Ross a parlé de la nécessité de ce qu'il appelle des amputations radicales en médecine. Le Dr Sam Rabinovitch a suggéré l'existence de ce qu'on pourrait appeler « cancer social ». Ils insistent tous deux pour qu'on entreprenne une lutte commune contre le problème de l'enfant maltraité et de la « famille difficile, à multiple problèmes ». Pourquoi pas ? Pourquoi ne pas étudier ce qui pourrait se faire dans les diverses villes du Canada et prendre les mesures voulues pour que ce soit fait.

Enfin, je parlerai du travail à effectuer sur la communauté. Que l'on pense en termes de ce que fait localement Ed Smee dans le comté Lanark en Ontario, des efforts qui se font au Manitoba pour aider la population indienne, ou de l'important projet A.R.D.A.-B.A.E.Q. en Gaspésie, voilà le genre d'innovations sociales qui offrent des possibilités immenses. Je suis extrêmement intéressé par tout cela et le mois prochain, je pars pour sept mois au Mexique, au Pérou, à Porto-Rico, et tenterai d'y apprendre quelque chose. J'espère ramener de nombreuses notes que je mettrai à la disposition du public à mon retour. Je suis certain que dans notre pays soit-disant si en avance, nous pourrions apprendre beaucoup en abordant nos propres régions sous-développées avec le point de vue des pays soi-disant arriérés.

Sixièmement... et notre Conférence canadienne de l'enfance ? C'est intentionnellement que je laisse ici un point d'interrogation. On a préparé des propositions précises qu'il vous faudra étudier ce soir au cours de réunions de comités provinciaux et discuter à la réunion générale de jeudi.

En conclusion, puis-je vous demander de vous reporter au discours d'inauguration du Dr Alva Myrdal, dimanche soir, et aux remarques profondes faites par le Dr Alan Thomas mardi matin, disant que la compétence ne suffit pas si nous voulons atteindre les buts que nous nous sommes fixés. Compassion, dévouement, perception, sont encore plus importants. Ce que le Dr Alan Gregg de la fondation Rockefeller a dit en parlant de la médecine s'applique à toutes les autres professions qui sont au service de l'humanité : « Les erreurs qui se commettent en médecine ne sont pas le fait d'ignorants, mais d'indifférents ».

Review and Commentary: III

DR. ALAN THOMAS

My task today is somewhat different, for the report of your discussions yesterday will be reflected in the report of the Conclusions Committee which follows. Instead, I am going to consider the Conference as a whole—particularly as it was viewed by some of our distinguished guests. Since so much of our national business in Canada is now carried out in conference, it seemed to me that it would be helpful to reflect on some aspects of this Conference—on some of its enormous successes and on some of its near ones.

One of our international visitors commented on the attractive size of this Conference, on the fact that it was manageable. Perhaps this is as much a result of the size of our population as of the skill with which the participants were chosen. In any event, I was challenged to wonder whether we capitalize enough on the quality, inherent in Canadian life, which comes with a relatively small population. Do we really exploit the possibility for activity and understanding and unified action that this provides?

A second, and most consistent, comment was on the range of participation—not only geographically—but also in terms of the kinds of interests, and the disciplines that are represented among the delegates. It is worth remembering that with this variety of approaches and professional viewpoints you have been able to practice inter-disciplinary communication as well as to consider the need for it.

This inter-disciplinary nature of the Conference has been one of its exciting aspects. It has made possible the focussing of a wealth of resources at the point where co-operation is the most necessary—on behalf of children. This is unique because as professions and specialized groups we tend to organize on our own lines not only nationally but internationally and we need opportunities for new ways of responding to problems and deploying our resources.

One significant comment was that we have both old and new professions represented here. For new professions that have been struggling to achieve status and reasonable prestige, co-operation may seem more difficult than for those professions that are well established and that have no "rear-guard action still to fight." It is useful to reflect on the fact that we all live in our own historical context and there are a variety of professional histories and a variety of professional stages of development represented here.

Another consistent comment was about the validity or value of the group experience. A number of people were puzzled by what could be accomplished—by what the results might be—but found the process interesting. The fact is that whatever the outcome of the Conference, many of you are going away with a greater understanding of other professions, other disciplines, other areas of interest which were previously mysteries. I think that a phrase that we used to use when I was a child best describes what has taken place: the act of "learning by heart." When little children say this they mean to memorize in order to be able to repeat what they have learned. But in the classical sense, it means that we have learned something so well that it is automatically translated into action. Perhaps "learning by heart" describes the potential of the group process in which we have all engaged.

One comment from our international guests suggests very forcibly that we need to examine our practices. In discussion we appear to qualify our descriptive statements. We say "that may be so in British Columbia or Manitoba but we don't do things that way in Nova Scotia," or "yes, that's the way it happens in Alberta but what do we do about it in Quebec?" Our comments left our visitors wondering if there was such a thing as a "Canadian" child. I think we need to be aware of the degree to which our practices on behalf of children, focussed as they are by provincial and regional responsibility, may make it difficult to help children to feel a part of the larger Canadian community. The enormous importance of the voluntary organization which can give some national interpretation and focus in areas of provincial governmental responsibility should not be overlooked. Perhaps one of the important aspects of this Conference is that it is one of the major voices speaking for children as Canadian children, rather than as children of one province or another.

I feel I must make one critical comment. I do not find that we, as a responsible adult population concerned with the life and vitality of our country, have put enough imagination into solving the problem of handling two languages in small group discussion. We can depend on electronic apparatus for our large meetings, but the situation in small groups, where the business of our country is really conducted, is more difficult. I don't believe we have learned yet how to free our French-speaking citizens from the double burden of performing responsibly and actively in two languages. I think the desire and intention was here—but I hope that in future national conferences we will search even harder for new and imaginative approaches to one of our most pressing national problems. Because of the frustration encountered, I think we have not been able to take full advantage of the laboratory that Quebec provides. What is happening to youth in Quebec is in many ways more exciting, more concrete in its variety than in any other province in Canada. There is much to be learned, not about, but from, Quebec. Some of our inhibitions, difficulties, and frustrations in dealing with two languages have obscured some of the dynamic experiences that are here for all to see and appreciate.

One last comment—this has been a very non-sentimental conference. While we have been trying to make the protection of the rights of small children commensurate with their individuality and their integrity, there has been little attempt to protect, or overprotect other groups of "the young." When we talked about youth, there has been a very real interest in sharing our worlds—and this, it seems to me, is a highly admirable characteristic for the kind of discussion in which we have been engaged.

This absence of sentiment allows me to introduce some in closing and to remind you that, in our concern for maturity for our children, growing-up is the one thing that we cannot stop. We can shape and help and share in the way in which they grow—but they will grow up regardless of what we do. In admitting that a child has an integrity of his or her own, I recognize a further concern expressed in the following lines, which I find comforting at times:

I sigh that kiss you
For I must own
That I will miss you
When you are grown.

Revue et commentaire: III

AUJOURD'HUI MA TÂCHE est quelque peu différente, car le rapport sur vos discussions d'hier sera incorporé dans le rapport du comité des conclusions, qui va suivre. Aujourd'hui, je veux étudier le congrès dans son ensemble, et surtout avec les yeux de nos hôtes distingués, venus de l'étranger. Puisque notre congrès s'est tellement occupé de l'état de nos affaires au Canada, il me semble qu'il serait utile de nous arrêter sur certains de ses aspects, sur quelques-unes de ses grandes réussites, et les « presque réussites ».

Un de ces visiteurs étrangers a remarqué le nombre commode de participants à ce congrès. Nous n'étions pas trop nombreux. Peut-être est-ce dû au nombre de nos habitants tout au tant qu'au talent des délégués. Quoi qu'il en soit, cela m'a poussé à me demander si nous savons utiliser la qualité de vie qui, au Canada, va de pair avec une population relativement restreinte. Exploitons-nous vraiment le potentiel d'activité, de compréhension, d'action d'ensemble que cela nous permet ?

Un second commentaire, souvent entendu, a été la mesure de la participation non seulement géographiquement, mais aussi en termes d'intensité d'intérêt et du nombre de professions représentées. Il vaut la peine de se rappeler qu'avec cette variété de points de vue et de méthodes professionnelles, vous avez pu mettre en pratique la collaboration professionnelle aussi bien qu'en étudier le besoin.

La nature inter-disciplines de ce congrès a été un de ses aspects les plus excitants. Cela a permis de réunir un nombre étonnant de ressources à l'endroit où la collaboration est le plus nécessaire, dans l'intérêt des enfants. C'est là une chose unique, parce que, en tant que professions et groupes spécialisés, nous avons tendance à nous organiser à notre façon non seulement sur le plan national, mais aussi international, et il nous faut trouver l'occasion de découvrir de nouvelles façons de résoudre les problèmes et d'employer nos ressources.

Un commentaire significatif portait sur le fait qu'il y a ici d'anciennes et de nouvelles disciplines. La coopération peut sembler plus difficile aux jeunes professions qui luttent pour obtenir le statut et le prestige qu'elles méritent, alors que les professions établies depuis plus longtemps n'ont pas besoin de « se battre avec l'arrière-garde ». Il est bon de penser que nous vivons tous dans un contexte historique et qu'il y a eu ici toute une variété d'histoires et d'époques professionnelles.

Un autre commentaire persistant a été la validité de l'expérience de groupe. Certains des assistants se sont demandé ce qu'on pouvait vraiment accomplir, ce que pourraient être les résultats ; mais ils ont trouvé l'expérience intéressante tout de même. Quel que soit le résultat final, c'est un fait acquis que la plupart d'entre vous repartiront avec une meilleure compréhension des autres professions, des autres disciplines et des autres secteurs d'intérêt qui étaient auparavant un mystère. Il me semble qu'une expression que nous utilisions lorsque j'étais enfant décrit le mieux ce qui s'est passé : « apprendre par cœur ». Les enfants, eux, veulent dire qu'ils ont appris de façon à pouvoir répéter leur leçon. Mais au sens classique de l'expression « apprendre par cœur », cela veut dire apprendre si bien qu'automatiquement les connaissances se traduisent en actes. Voilà qui décrit peut-être le plus clairement ce que peut offrir le travail de groupe auquel nous nous sommes livrés.

Un commentaire exprimé par un hôte étranger montre combien il est important que nous réexaminions nos façons de faire. Au cours des discussions, nous avons tendance à qualifier nos descriptions ! « Il en va peut-être ainsi en Colombie britannique, mais nous faisons autrement en Nouvelle-Ecosse ». Ou encore « Oui, bien sûr, cela se fait comme cela en Alberta, mais au Québec voilà ce que nous faisons ». Et nos visiteurs finissaient par se demander s'il existait vraiment une enfance canadienne. Il faut prendre conscience de la mesure dans laquelle nos façons d'agir, centrées sur nos responsabilités provinciales ou régionales en matière d'enfance, peuvent empêcher les enfants de sentir qu'ils sont membres d'une communauté beaucoup plus vaste, le Canada. L'importance énorme du bénévolat, qui peut donner une perspective et une interprétation nationales à des responsabilités provinciales, ne doit pas être négligée. Un des aspects les plus importants de la Conférence canadienne de l'enfance, c'est qu'elle est un des interprètes les plus importants de l'enfance canadienne, et non de l'enfance d'une province ou d'une autre.

Il me faut toutefois vous soumette une critique. J'estime que, en tant que population adulte et soucieuse de la vie et de la vitalité du Canada, nous n'avons pas suffisamment mis notre imagination à l'épreuve quand il s'est agi des deux langues, dans les petits groupes. Nous pouvions compter sur les appareils électroniques lors de grands sessions, mais dans les petits groupes, où se discutaient les affaires vraiment importantes pour le pays, c'était plus difficile. Je ne crois pas que nous ayons encore appris comment libérer nos compatriotes francophones du fardeau de se comporter de façon active et responsable en deux langues. L'intention était là, mais j'espère que lors des prochains congrès nationaux, nous chercherons des solutions nouvelles et plus imaginatives à l'un de nos plus pressants problèmes nationaux. A cause de la frustration qui en est résultée, je ne pense pas que nous ayons pleinement profité du laboratoire que nous offre le Québec. Ce qui arrive à la jeunesse du Québec est de bien des façons plus excitant, plus concret, plus varié que dans les autres provinces. Il y a beaucoup à apprendre non pas sur le Québec, mais du Québec. Nos inhibitions, nos difficultés ont obscurci certaines des expériences dynamiques que nous aurions tous pu voir et apprécier.

Un dernier commentaire : ce congrès a fait très peu de place à la sentimentalité. Bien que nous ayons essayé de protéger les droits des tout jeunes enfants à la mesure de leur individualité et de leur intégrité, nous n'avons pas essayé de protéger ou de surprotéger les autres catégories de jeunes. Quand nous avons parlé de la jeunesse, nous avons manifesté un réel désir de partager nos univers, et cela, me semble-t-il, est une des caractéristiques les plus admirables du genre de discussions que nous avons entreprises.

Cette absence de sentimentalité me permet de vous dire, en terminant, que, lorsque nous nous préoccupons de la maturité de nos enfants, la croissance est un phénomène que nous ne pouvons pas empêcher. Nous pouvons former, aider, participer à la façon dont la croissance s'effectue, mais, quoi que nous fassions, elle s'effectuera.

Et en reconnaissant à un enfant sa propre intégrité, voilà que naît un autre souci, bien traduit dans les vers suivants, que j'ai parfois trouvé consolants :

> I sigh that kiss you
> For I must own
> That I will miss you
> When you are grown.*

*En t'embrassant je soupire / Car il faut bien le dire / Tu me manqueras tant / Quand tu seras grand.

Report of the Conclusions Committee

DR. J. F. McCREARY

My work in the last few years has taken me away from pediatrics and the allied professions, and it was therefore particularly pleasant for me to be invited to this Conference to have an opportunity of renewing old friendships and old interests which are still very strong. I am particularly proud of having had the opportunity of chairing the Conclusions Committee whose members were Dr. Alan Ross, Dr. Reva Gerstein, Dr. Sam Rabinovitch, Dr. Keith Armstrong, Professor Charles Hendry, and Mrs. Mabel Taylor. They have been a wonderful committee to work with not just on this occasion but over a good many years.

I would like to present our report this morning as briefly and as factually as I can, and to present it in two parts. The first part represents a series of principles, which your Conclusions Committee felt could be said to have been reached by this Conference.

1. Any problem which impedes progress to maturity cannot be solved by any one professional group alone. I believe that this came out of the Conference loud and clear. It has not come out at any of the previous conferences with which we have been concerned.

2. This being true, it follows that in the training for each profession there must be included a component which involves inter-professional collaboration and experience: Health is not solely the problem for the physician; education is not only the terrain of professional teachers; welfare is not the prerogative solely of the social worker. I think this, too, became forcibly apparent to us.

3. It follows that the significant number of professionals in many communities should increase their cumulative impact on the problems of children by forming multi-disciplinary working groups. And about this, I shall have more to say later.

4. It will be necessary to use much greater imagination in finding ways of creating a more effective deployment of professional person-

nel such as doctors and social workers in rural areas, teachers in slum areas and all the other variants with which you are familiar. You are familiar too with how serious are the problems which lack of such people presents to providing opportunities for Canadian children.

5. This is a bold statement but we believe it to be true that it will not be possible to prepare sufficient professionals to meet the needs of children in the future. And I would add that in the face of rapidly increasing knowledge, in the face of increasing sophistication on the part of our population, and increasing demands, we do not believe we can train the professionals to do the job. Further, it is probably a more desirable alternative to share some of these functions now performed by professionals among other individuals.

6. Under these circumstances, it becomes the duty of professionally trained individuals and the policy makers to analyze community needs and methods of utilizing semi-professional and non-professional individuals with appropriate preparation. Any new training programme should develop through the collaboration of universities, community colleges, technical institutes, extension departments, and community agencies. We have been used to orientating our training through universities but we must become aware of the rapidly expanding number and range of facilities that are becoming available to us. If we do not make full use of this range, we will not train the people we require.

7. The volunteer should play a much greater role in the provision of services to children in the future than he has in the past. If we are to develop sufficient numbers of volunteers much more imaginative approaches must be made in attracting, preparing, and using them. With the acceleration of automation there will be a vast number of people with expanded non-working time which could well be spent in volunteer services. And here is an area in which we firmly believe we must exert much more imaginative effort than we have in the past.

8. We are very concerned with the inequality of educational opportunity among Canadian children and we are equally concerned that conditioning forces within the home and within the environment limit the ability of some children to profit from the normal educational opportunities.

9. We believe that any parent or guardian whose child is refused an educational opportunity by a local school board, for any reason whatever, must have access to a neutral tribunal for review. As you know this is not now the case, nor are the decisions always just.

10. We support the stand of teacher-training colleges that the

present duration of training is in most instances inadequate to provide all the skills and understandings which teachers must possess.

11. Canada's effort in basic and applied research in the social sciences has been pitifully small. It is urgent that both financial support for such studies and opportunities for preparation of research personnel be made available. In this connection we welcome the indication that the Vanier Institute on the Family will substantially support such research.

As an aside, I think I should say that I think the second of those two requirements is more serious than the first. If we did have the funds immediately, we simply don't have the trained workers that could go to work in these fields.

12. A positive and open-minded approach is urgently needed if we are to join with young adults, and the use of that term, rather than youth or teenagers is deliberate, to meet the challenges which they face. Obviously this is a major problem about which we have said only a few words.

The Conclusions Committee felt we could say these things with reasonable assurance because they arose out of the recommendations which came from your groups.* I would like to outline, statistically and otherwise, the nature, number, and weight of the recommendations your twenty-five groups produced yesterday.

As you know, each of the groups was asked to prepare anywhere from two to four statements or recommendations. All produced at least four. Some found it difficult in their enthusiasm to stop at four, and we ended up with significantly more than 100 recommendations or statements.

It was very clear that there were three major areas on which opinion was unanimous in every group. The first and foremost among these was your very serious concern about the problems of communication between the various professional groups which are concerned with children. In this regard, I note a marked change in attitude since the first conference at the Seaway Hotel in Toronto, back in 1957. At the time of that conference we were not at all sure that this interdisciplinary communication would work. We were afraid that we would encounter such explosive differences of opinions and philosophies that this might well break down. We were surprised when the small group of us that were there found that we could indeed indulge in conversation of the

*An edited version of these recommendations can be obtained by writing the Canadian Council on Children and Youth, 165 Bloor St. E., suite 302, Toronto 5.

sort that we have been engaged in for the last three days: that it was not only possible but useful for we had all profited by the experience. So some of us left the Seaway Conference with the feeling that this was important. In the three years that elapsed between the conferences of 1957 and 1960 provincial and local multi-disciplinary committees were at work and the concept of this type of an approach gradually spread.

But still, in 1960 it would not have been possible to have the conference agree that the lack of such communication was one of the problems, if not the major one, facing the development of childhood in Canada today. Even in 1960 there were a fair number of us who were not completely sure where we were going with this inter-disciplinary movement. However, on the very opening day of this conference, we did not ask whether or not this was a problem, it was a question of solving it. This came out of every single group. We actually had thirty-one recommendations on this particular subject from your twenty-five groups, so some felt it strongly enough to express it a second time. I can't help feeling that this represents real progress.

What does it mean in terms of the activities of the Canadian Conference on Children? Are we simply riding an awakening interest and recognition of a problem that has always been there, or are we beginning to see the results of the communication that has taken place over the years at the provincial and at the local level? I feel the latter plays a very prominent part in this change of view which is so obvious to those of us who have had the opportunity of following this movement from the beginning. When one examined the thirty-one recommendations, it became clear that for most of the groups an immediate solution should be attempted, by beginning to integrate the various professional groups at the local level. You pointed out in most of your recommendations that in many communities you now have quite a responsible cadre of professionally trained individuals, but that as long as they were working in isolation they were not producing their greatest cumulative effect. You didn't believe that this was likely to be solved by an agency, which normally employed just social workers, suddenly taking on the part or fulltime services of a dentist or a physician. You laid responsibility on the professionals themselves, and recommended that, regardless of the agency for which they work, they get together and continue to communicate in relation to planning for community facilities and in relation to meeting the problems raised by schools and other institutions in the community.

One group illustrated their recommendation by describing a pattern that had been developed. In a relatively small community some time ago it was arranged that, at monthly intervals, the director of the health services, the principal of the school, the counsellors of the school, the public health nurses, and the director of welfare would sit down and review the incipient or the obvious developments of abnormalities in children within the school system and bring their combined weight of knowledge and professional skill to bear in an attempt to alleviate these at this time. This was the pattern that seemed to go through so many of these recommendations. Let us make use of the experiences we have had in these conferences with the people that we now have in our community. We thought, in our committee, that this was a healthy, sane approach; that it was responsible of you not to simply demand more and more trained personnel or more and more funds for this purpose, but rather to say "let's make use of what we have."

Another group recommended another approach to the problem. A small but very significant number of recommendations were directed towards the professional training schools, and they outlined the need for joint teaching of undergraduate professionals in order that sympathy and an understanding of both the abilities and accomplishments and the problems of the other professional groups would be recognized.

I have been asked so many times about what we are trying to do at the University of British Columbia in this regard, that I am going to take about three minutes to try to say something about it now. We have a relatively new medical school and we had to build new facilities which would, to a degree, cement forever the personality and the nature of the school. So we took some time to look at the changes in the provision of health sciences which might affect the nature of the facilities that we were preparing. One which was clearly recognizable was the rapidly changing role of the physician. Whereas 40 years ago he was virtually the sole purveyor of health services, now he has been joined by a large number of professional groups—groups that have formed their own professional societies, developed their own teaching staffs, learned their own vocabulary, and developed their own goals, and that are just about as widely separated as is possible. It seemed to us that it was very difficult to bring these groups together unless they had some shared experience, unless they had some reason to believe that they had knowledge of what the others knew and could accomplish. So we are developing a health sciences centre, rather than a university hospital, which will provide the same teaching facilities, staff, and patients for medical students, dental students, pharmacy students, nursing students, students in rehabilitation medicine, clinical psychologists, social workers, and dieticians; in short, the whole gambit of people who work together in the field of mental, emotional, and physical health.

The way in which their teaching is to be integrated is something which we are working through at the present time. One might oversimplify and say that it occurs at three levels.

First of all, there is a body of knowledge concerning health, particularly community health and the mobilization of community resources, which every person in the field of health should have, whether he be a trained brain surgeon or a dental hygienist. This will be taught to all, in groups of 400 or 500 people by the best teacher available: it may be a social worker, it may be a clinical psychologist, or it may be a dentist.

Secondly, in the basic medical sciences it is clear that all the people who are involved in any of the health professions should have some knowledge of the professional entities of physiology, bio-chemistry, anatomy, pharmacology, and the like. And so, in addition to the detailed course made available to medical students and the less detailed course for students in the second or third year of the science faculty, a third course of a survey nature has been developed, which will permit people to come in contact with these departments to learn their philosophy and their vocabulary.

Finally, and this cannot come into effect until the facilities are complete in 1969, we believe that the clinical teaching of these people should take place again in groups representing the different disciplines. We have traditionally taught our medical students with clinics of six or eight people and an instructor. How much more effective it would be if we could introduce for a part of that clinical training, a clinic with a medical student, a dental student, a pharmacy student, a nurse, and a representative from each of the health groups. This is obviously not the whole answer, by any manner of means, but it might, and perhaps will, create a climate in which professional groups can work more closely together.

Thus, the most important problem with which you were concerned in your groups yesterday was the problem of lack of communication and understanding between the professions. When different opinions are given by different professional groups the result is confusion for parents and roadblocks to normal maturity.

The second problem, drawing a recommendation from all of your twenty-five groups, had to do with education. But the recommendations and explorations concerning education were varied in the extreme. I want to read the preamble to one of the recommendations exactly as it came from one of the groups because it expresses the philosophy which ran through many of the recommendations. This states: "Until now education has been too much a function of the goals of success for a materialistic society and hence has failed to turn out an individual who is wise, mature, and concerned. In the past, education has been too pragmatic and too technical; it has been geared to preserve too much the static traditions of the past. We must now make education serve to honour the living traditions of the past, to help the youth and adults of the world achieve the fullest degree of individual growth and development, to reach out in service and care for all mankind." This I believe, could be regarded as a general statement of belief that provides a preamble for your more specific recommendations.

The most frequent request—coming from six of your twenty-five groups—was for more education in family life. This was not confined to the formal school system, but many of the recommendations felt that training for family life should be increased in the school and could be, if the teachers were more adequately prepared to present it.

Four of the groups stated that they wished to see the curriculum stress creativity to a greater degree. This produced a certain amount of discussion among your committee and we wondered whether the real plea was not for a school environment in which the individual student and his abilities were identifiable and identified, and in which there were teachers who were imaginative and independent in their approach to their task.

There were four groups who recommended that teachers' training give them more understanding of the problems of the development of children and a greater ability to recognize deviations from normal. This specific recommendation was touched on by a number of other groups in various ways. There were two groups that stressed the need for a greater equality of opportunity for children in different schools, and although the greatest amount of discussion related to the rural versus the urban school, nonetheless the school in the slum district was touched on and very real concern was expressed with regard to the highly special and very difficult problems of meeting the needs of Indian and Eskimo children.

There were two groups who referred to counselling in the school system. They requested a different type of training for counsellors to permit a greater understanding and a more effective level of counselling.

Several groups recommended that more of the services for children be attached to the school; that more screening services be provided to detect minor deviations in physical, mental, and emotional health. This made good sense to your committee. Until the child reaches the school system there is no chance to evaluate him in comparison with his peers, and, therefore, the opportunity for picking up deviations in any direction becomes infinitely greater as soon as the child enters the school system. So it was felt important to try to encourage the development of professional groups around the school system so that when these deviations were detected, the professional groups would be able to move in to assist.

Here is where we turn back to your strong recommendation that the local professionals form a multi-disciplinary group. Surely, the logical place for these groups is the school making it possible for their specific professional abilities to assist in solving problems as they arise among young children. We talk about problems as though they were only the defects found in those children who are identified as being unusual, but it is as important to pick up and recognize early the very talented child and to put him into the programme in which he can use his talents.

One of the groups presented the interesting recommendation that there be a very much greater international content in the curriculum, particularly in the primary school system. They felt that Canadian children should be made much more aware of themselves as related to children in other nations; that the national identity which would be desirable for our children would be much more readily obtained if we taught them more about children in other parts of the world. Your committee felt that this was an imaginative recommendation.

One group, and, surprisingly, one group only, spoke about the need for continuing education, particularly for the professional groups. In my own profession this has been a very strongly recognized need for some time, and it has been stated that a doctor arises each morning a little bit less effective because of the advances that have been made in medicine during the time he slept.

The World Health Organization has recently issued some very startling figures. There are over 50,000 medical journals in the world today publishing over 1,200,000 articles a year, a new article in the field of medicine every 23 seconds. So continuing medical education has been a matter of great concern, so much so that the twelve medical schools in Canada have officially accepted this as one of their stated responsibilities, quite as important as undergraduate medical education. And I suspect that this need in the other professional groups will increase very markedly. The reason why this is true in medicine is because we have been able to get funds for research and it is this vastly expanded research effort, over the past twenty years or thereabouts, that has produced this flood of new information. When the funds that were referred to earlier become available in similar amounts for research in the social sciences, the advances will become so rapid that continuing education will, I think, be necessary for all of us.

The third area of almost unanimous concern, was the subject of volunteers. Twenty-three of your twenty-five groups recommended that greater use be made of volunteer services. It was stressed that in addition to providing for increased manpower, this would provide an added interest for people who perhaps do not have sufficient interests at the present time.

It was felt that we had to re-examine very carefully our use of volunteers and be much more imaginative. Although the woman whose family had grown up was frequently mentioned, particularly the highly educated one who may be bored and for whom life is relatively meaningless, strangely enough the group that was accented most in your recommendations was youth. The reason, of course, was that this provided a two-edged sword—not only did the older teenagers provide an addition to the work force, but also they themselves were learning about family living during the course of providing this service.

Most of the twenty-three recommendations that were received stressed that in the term "volunteer" they were covering many varieties of workers. They were including some workers who had received a very significant amount of training; others that were completely untrained; workers who were full-time and partially remunerated or fully remunerated, and workers who were working part-time and receiving no remuneration. The point made by Sam Rabinovitch the other day—that there was a great new source of manpower which could be explored when automation reduces the work week and the working hours of individuals—came out in one or two of the recommendations which you made.

The unanimity of the opinions in these three different areas was really quite striking to us. But this is where it ended. The remainder of the recommendations are varied and only sparsely supported in the various groups. For example, there were five groups that were quite concerned about the problems of communication between the generations and these same five groups recommended that we certainly should have had children at this Conference, or at least young adult or the youth delegates. Under the heading of communications also there were a number of groups that attacked our present failure to use mass media imaginatively for the education of parents. They felt that we could be doing far, far more than we are in education of parents if we used radio and television more effectively than we now do. Your committee wondered about this. How much education occurs when the individual on the receiving end does not have any chance to participate?

There was some feeling about the need for planned families and there were five groups that specifically requested that section 150 of the Canadian Criminal Code should be amended to permit the legal distribution of contraceptive information and also of contraceptive devices.

Many of you are concerned about research. Twelve of the twenty-five groups reported on something related to research. There were six groups who simply stated the need for more research generally. There were two groups who raised the specific problem of the needs of the home and the needs of the family and the necessity of sociological and psychological research in this area; there were two that specifically mentioned the problems of children, and particularly of youth; and there were two groups that felt that the whole education process required a great deal more research than had been devoted to it.

You struggled with values, as did your Committee. Two groups stressed that the rights of children must take priority over the rights of parents. And two groups recommended that a sub-committee be set up to establish a meaningful examination and development of a statement of values for children.

You gave quite a lot of consideration to the next conference. Seven specific recommendations came in that there should be another Canadian Conference on Children, three of those suggesting that the next conference should be in a period of two years. Six suggested that there be continuing provincial conferences and projects between now and the next conference. Three suggested that the provinces begin work on the development of a charter for Canadian children—something that would be worked on in the interval between now and the next conference and which could be adopted at that time. And three reiterated that they wanted to have participation by youth in the next conference.

A number of your groups were disturbed at the similarities of purpose of the Vanier Institute on the Family and the Canadian Conference on Children. Five of your groups produced a specific recommendation that either amalgamation of these two groups or the closest possible co-operation and integration be explored and effected if possible.

Two groups wished to see a permanent secretariat set up by the Canadian Conference on Children to promote action at governmental and local levels and to conduct and support research in other areas.

In short, your minds ranged actively over the problems of the "Road to Maturity." You identified roadblocks and made sane and solid recommendations concerning their removal. The surprising thing to all of us was the complete unanimity of your concern and identification of the three major areas: the inter-professional communication, the re-examination of our educational patterns, and the increased use of our volunteers. I know that I speak for those who organized this Conference when I say how grateful they are for the interest, the energy, and the wisdom which you have demonstrated these last three days.

Although this is a report of the Conclusions Committee, it can't help, to some degree, being a description of the Conference and as such it fails abjectly. How could one produce a distillate at this time which contains these various ingredients: the great wisdom that shone through the simple statements made by Dr. Myrdal on Sunday night; the straightforward, thoughtful charge laid upon us by Dr. Alan Ross on Monday morning; the brilliant running commentary brought to us daily by Dr. Alan Thomas and the dramatic searching direction given to us by Dr. Sam Rabinovitch and Professor C. E. Hendry. These things can only be remembered.

As the Conference draws to a close, let us not forget the monumental and effective work done by the interdisciplinary groups at the provincial and at the local levels in preparation for it. In a sense, this Conference is just a window which lets us look at what has gone on provincially and locally and at some of the effects of this work. It is this on-going effort which I am sure will continue to change the attitude towards children by the professionals and others who are engaged in their care. I hope that you are proud, as I am proud, to have had a little part in the Second Canadian Conference on Children.

J. F. MCCREARY

Rapport du comité des conclusions

MES TRAVAUX au cours de ces dernières années m'ont éloigné de la pédiatrie, et des professions qui s'y rattachent, et c'est par conséquent d'autant plus agréable pour moi d'être invité à ce congrès, de renouer de vieilles amitiés et de me pencher à nouveau sur des problèmes qui n'ont jamais cessé de m'intéresser. Je suis tout particulièrement fier d'avoir été appelé à diriger le comité des conclusions, qui se compose du Dr Alan Ross, du Dr Reva Gerstein, du Dr Sam Rabinovitch, du Dr Keith Armstrong, du Professeur Charles Hendry et de Mme Mabel Taylor. Voilà un comité avec lequel il a été passionnant de travailler, non seulement en cette occasion, mais pendant plusieurs années.

Je voudrais vous soumettre mon rapport aussi brièvement et aussi précisément que possible, et vous le présenter en deux parties. La première partie représente une série de principes que, d'après le comité des conclusions, ce congrès a formulé.

1. Les problèmes qui empêchent le processus normal de maturation ne peuvent être résolus par un seul groupe professionnel. Je crois que nous en avons plus clairement pris conscience à ce congrès qu'en aucune autre occasion.

2. Ceci étant admis, il s'ensuit que dans la formation à toutes les professions il doit rentrer un élément consacré à l'expérience et à la collaboration interprofessionnelle : la santé ne regarde pas seulement le médecin ; l'éducation ne concerne pas seulement les enseignants ; le bien-être n'est pas le domaine exclusif du travailleur social. Il me semble que cela aussi s'est fait clairement sentir.

3. Il s'ensuit que les professionnels, dans bien des cas, pourraient amplifier l'importance cumulative de leurs efforts en formant des équipes de travail multi-disciplines. Je reviendrai sur ce sujet tout à l'heure.

4. Il devient nécessaire de nous servir davantage de notre imagination pour trouver le moyen de mieux déployer nos ressources en personnel professionnel, par exemple d'envoyer des médecins et des travailleurs sociaux dans les régions rurales, des professeurs dans les quartiers misérables, et autres secteurs d'activité que vous connaissez bien. Vous savez également combien sérieux sont les problèmes que représente l'absence de tels services pour les enfants canadiens.

5. Nous ne pensons pas trop nous avancer en disant qu'il sera impossible de former suffisamment de professionnels pour subvenir aux besoins des enfants dans l'avenir. A cela j'ajoute que, devant l'augmentation des connaissances, devant la sophistication croissante de la population et devant les exigences qui se multiplient sans cesse, nous ne pensons pas que la solution soit la formation de plus de professionnels. Et il vaut sans doute mieux partager certains rôles joués jusqu'ici par les professionnels avec d'autres.

6. En raison de ces circonstances, tous les individus jouissant d'une formation professionnelle et tous ceux qui dictent les lignes de conduite dans la société ont le devoir d'analyser les besoins de la communauté et les moyens d'utiliser les services des semi-professionnels et des non-professionnels qui ont la formation voulue. Tout nouveau programme de formation devrait se faire en collaboration entre universités, collèges, instituts techniques, services d'extension et agences locales. Nous sommes tellement habitués à envisager la formation sur le plan universitaire qu'il nous faut absolument prendre conscience du nombre et de la variété des possibilités de formation qui s'offrent à nous. Sinon nous ne pourrons former le personnel dont nous avons besoin.

7. Il faut que, à l'avenir, le bénévole joue un plus grand rôle dans les services consacrés à l'enfance qu'il ne l'a fait dans le passé. Si nous voulons l'aide de nombreux bénévoles, il nous faudra davantage d'imagination pour les attirer, les former et utiliser leurs services. Avec l'accélération de l'automation, il va y avoir toute une catégorie d'individus dont le temps libre pourrait être employé à faire du bénévolat. Et c'est là un secteur où nous estimons qu'il faut utiliser beaucoup plus d'imagination que dans le passé.

8. Nous sommes très préoccupés par l'inégalité des possibilités d'éducation offertes aux enfants canadiens. Nous sommes également soucieux de ce que les éléments déterminants à la maison et dans le milieu limitent les capacités qu'auraient certains enfants de profiter des possibilités normales d'éducation.

9. Nous estimons que tout parent ou tuteur dont l'enfant se voit refuser la possibilité de s'instruire par une commission scolaire quelconque, quelque soit la raison, doit pouvoir prier un tribunal impartial d'étudier la question. Comme vous le savez, il n'en va pas ainsi en ce moment, et les décisions sont souvent injustes.

10. Nous sommes d'accord avec les écoles normales qui estiment que la période de formation actuelle est insuffisante et, la plupart du

temps, ne permet pas de donner aux instituteurs les connaissances et la compréhension dont ils ont besoin.

11. Les efforts canadiens dans le domaine de la recherche appliquée en sciences sociales sont maigres. Il est urgent que des subsides à ces travaux soient accordés et qu'un personnel de recherches soit formé. Nous sommes heureux, à ce propos, de noter que l'Institut Vanier de la famille semble devoir apporter une aide substantielle à ces travaux.

J'ajouterai, pour ma part, que le second de ces points me paraît le plus important. Même si nous obtenions tout de suite des fonds, nous n'avons pas le personnel voulu pour travailler à ces recherches.

12. Une façon ouverte et positive d'aborder le problème est des plus nécessaires si nous voulons nous unir aux jeunes adultes (et nous préférons ce terme à celui de jeunesse ou d'adolescents), pour faire face à leurs problèmes. C'est là visiblement un très grand sujet que nous avons à peine abordé.

Le Comité des conclusions estime pouvoir parler ainsi sans trop de crainte de se tromper, car toutes ces réflexions naissent des recommandations énoncées par vos groupes*. Je voudrais vous donner, du point de vue statistique, et en général, une idée de la nature, du nombre et du poids des recommandations que vos vingt-cinq groupes ont rédigées hier.

Comme vous le savez, on a prié chaque groupe de préparer de deux à quatre déclarations ou recommandations. Tous en ont rédigé au moins quatre. Certains, dans leur enthousiasme, ont trouvé difficile de se borner là. En fin de compte, on nous a remis plus de cent recommandations.

Il est évident que l'unanimité règne dans trois grands secteurs. Le premier, le principal, c'est votre grave souci de communication entre les différents groupes professionnels qui travaillent dans le domaine de l'enfance. A cet égard, j'ai remarqué un net changement d'attitude depuis la première conférence au Seaway Hotel de Toronto, en 1958. A cette époque-là, nous n'étions pas sûrs d'obtenir des résultats du point de vue interprofessionnel. Nous avions peur de nous heurter à de telles différences d'opinions et de philosophies, à des dissentiments tellement explosifs que les communications s'arrêteraient immédiatement. Nous avons été surpris lorsque le petit groupe d'entre nous qui s'était réuni là s'est aperçu qu'on pouvait vraiment se parler comme nous nous sommes parlé au cours de ces trois dernières journées. Et

*On peut se procurer un exemplaire revu et corrigé de ces recommandations en s'adressant au CCEJ, 165 Bloor St. E., suite 302, Toronto 5.

que ce n'était pas seulement possible, mais utile, et que l'expérience servait à tous. Certains sont repartis du Congrès du Seaway avec le sentiment que ces rapports étaient vraiment importants. Au cours des deux années qui se sont écoulées entre les congrès de 1958 et de 1960, des comités locaux et provinciaux « multi-disciplines » ont travaillé et l'idée de ce genre de travail s'est graduellement répandue.

Mais pourtant, en 1960, le congrès n'aurait pu admettre que le problème de communication était un des problèmes les plus importants, sinon le plus important, dans le domaine du développement de l'enfance canadienne. Même en 1960, certains d'entre nous se demandaient où nous pouvions en venir avec cette collaboration interprofessionnelle. Toutefois, dès l'ouverture de ce congrès, il n'a pas été question de se demander si le problème existait, mais seulement : comment le résoudre. Et cela s'est retrouvé dans chaque groupe. Il y a eu trente et une recommandations sur le sujet, provenant des vingt-cinq groupes. Autrement dit, certains groupes sont tellement persuadés de l'importance du sujet qu'ils ont jugé bon d'y revenir deux fois.

Qu'est-ce que cela signifie du point de vue des activités de la Conférence canadienne de l'enfance ? Partageons-nous simplement la prise de conscience d'un problème qui a toujours existé, ou commençons-nous de voir les résultats de cette communication qui a eu lieu au cours des dernières années sur le plan provincial et sur le plan local ? Il me semble que ce dernier élément a joué un rôle très important dans ce changement d'opinion qui parait tellement évident à nous qui avons suivi le mouvement depuis le début. En examinant les trente et une recommandations, il devient évident que la plupart des groupes estiment indispensable de trouver une solution immédiate en commençant d'intégrer les différentes professions au niveau local. Vous avez fait ressortir dans la plupart de vos recommandations que dans beaucoup de localités il existe maintenant une pléiade de professionnels admirablement formés mais dont les efforts, parce qu'ils restent isolés, ne produisent pas l'effet cumulatif souhaitable. Vous n'estimez pas, dans ces textes, qu'on puisse y arriver en demandant à une agence qui jusqu'ici n'a employé que des travailleurs sociaux, d'engager tout d'un coup, à plein temps ou à mi-temps, les services d'un médecin ou d'un dentiste. La responsabilité, d'après vous, revient aux professionnels eux-mêmes. Et vous avez recommandé que, quelle que soit l'agence ou le service pour lesquels ils travaillent, ils se réunissent et continuent de communiquer en organisant les services de la localité et en faisant face aux problèmes scolaires ou autres de la localité.

Un groupe a illustré ses recommandations en décrivant ce qui s'est déjà fait. Dans une localité à la population relativement peu nombreuse, on a organisé, il y a quelque temps, des réunions mensuelles où siègent le directeur des services de santé, le principal de l'école, les orienteurs, les infirmières de santé publique et le directeur des services de bien-être, afin d'étudier les anomalies existantes ou en puissance chez les enfants du groupe scolaire, et de mettre leurs talents et leurs efforts en commun pour tenter d'y trouver remède. Voilà le type de solution qui est suggéré fréquemment dans les recommandations. Sachons mettre en pratique chez nous ce que ces congrès nous ont appris. Nous avons pensé, dans ce comité, qu'il s'agissait d'une façon saine et sensée d'envisager les problèmes et que c'est, de votre part, faire preuve de jugement et de sens des responsabilités que de ne pas réclamer davantage de personnel bien formé ou davantage de fonds, mais de vous dire « Servons-nous de ce que nous avons ».

Un autre groupe a recommandé une autre solution. Un petit nombre de recommandations – suffisamment toutefois pour qu'on y trouve de l'importance – s'adressaient aux grandes écoles où se donne la formation professionnelle, en soulignant le besoin d'un enseignement de base commun pour tous les étudiants non diplômés, afin que puisse naître la compréhension vis-à-vis des capacités, des résultats obtenus ou des problèmes des autres groupes professionnels.

On m'a demandé si souvent ce que nous faisons dans ce sens à l'University of British Columbia que je vais consacrer trois minutes à tenter de vous le décrire. Nous avons une école de médecine relativement récente, et ça a été à nous de créer ce qui, dans une certaine mesure, lui donnerait sa personnalité et son essence. Voilà pourquoi nous avons pris le temps d'étudier les changements qui, dans l'enseignement des sciences médicales, pourraient avoir une influence sur la nature de ce que nous voulions faire. Un des plus visibles, c'est l'évolution rapide du rôle du médecin. Alors qu'il y a seulement quarante ans, il était le seul praticien du domaine médical, il a vu le rejoindre toute une cohorte de groupes professionnels, des groupes qui ont formé leurs propres associations, établi leur propre corps professoral, appris leur propre vocabulaire et défini leurs propres buts, et qui sont aussi isolés qu'il est possible de l'être. Il nous a semblé qu'il était très difficile de rapprocher ces groupes, à moins qu'ils ne puissent partager quelques expériences, à moins de leur donner une raison de penser qu'ils savent ce que les autres connaissent et ce qu'ils peuvent accomplir. Aussi, ce qu'on a cherché à faire c'est de créer un centre de sciences sociales plutôt qu'un hôpital universitaire, qui sera chargé de l'enseignement avec le même personnel enseignant et les mêmes malades-cas, pour les étudiants en médecine, en dentisterie, en pharmacie, pour les élèves-infirmières, les étudiants en réadaptation, et en partie pour les futurs cliniciens en psychologie, travailleurs sociaux, diététiciennes ; en bref tout l'ensemble de ceux qui travaillent dans le domaine de la santé mentale, affective et physique.

La façon d'intégrer l'enseignement est le sujet de nos travaux du moment. On peut céder à la tentation de simplifier le problème et dire que cela peut se faire à trois niveaux.

D'abord, il y a un ensemble de connaissances sur la santé (particulièrement santé publique et mobilisation des ressources publiques) que doit posséder tout individu travaillant dans le domaine médical, fut-il neurochirurgien ou hygiéniste dentaire. Cela s'enseignera à tous les étudiants, par groupes de 450 ou 500 et le professeur sera la personne la plus compétente, travailleur social, psychologue, dentiste, etc.

Deuxièmement, quand il s'agit de sciences médicales de base, il est clair que toutes les personnes appartenant à ce genre de profession doivent avoir quelques connaissances en physiologie, bio-chimie, anatomie, pharmacologie et autres. Par conséquent, en plus du cours très détaillé destiné aux étudiants en médecine et du cours moins complet que suivent les étudiants de 2ième et 3ième année à la faculté des sciences, on a conçu un troisième cours de connaissances générales qui permettra aux étudiants de connaître tous ces secteurs, d'en apprendre la psychologie et le langage.

Finalement, et cela ne pourra se faire que lorsque les installations seront terminées en 1969, nous estimons que l'apprentissage clinique de ces étudiants devrait aussi se faire dans des groupes où sont représentées les diverses professions. Il est de tradition de former nos étudiants en médecine par cliniques de six ou huit, avec un instructeur. Combien plus efficace deviendrait la formation si nous pouvions créer, pour enseigner une partie des connaissances pratiques, des cliniques composées d'un étudiant en médecine, d'un futur dentiste, d'un futur pharmacien, d'une infirmière et d'un représentant de chacune des branches de la médecine.

Certainement ce n'est pas la seule solution, mais cela peut, nous l'espérons fort, créer une atmosphère dans laquelle les groupes professionnels peuvent collaborer ensemble plus étroitement.

Donc, le grand problème, d'après ce qu'ont fait savoir vos groupes hier, c'est le manque de communication et de compréhension entre les professions, résultant en opinions différentes données par des groupes professionnels différents, ce qui crée la confusion chez les parents et s'oppose au processus normal de la maturation.

Le second problème qui a attiré l'attention de vos vingt-cinq groupes concerne l'éducation. Mais les recommandations et les discussions à ce sujet varient à l'infini. Je veux vous lire le préambule à une de ces recommandations tel qu'il nous est parvenu du groupe qui l'a rédigé, parce qu'il traduit bien la philosophie de la plupart des groupes : « Jusqu'à présent l'éducation a été bien trop dirigée vers la réussite dans une société matérialiste et par conséquent n'a pas réussi à produire un individu mûr, sage, et soucieux des grands problèmes. Dans le passé l'éducation a été trop pragmatique, trop technique, elle a trop cherché à conserver les valeurs statiques du passé. Il faut que nous transformions le système éducatif, pour servir les traditions vivantes du passé, pour aider les jeunes et les adultes du monde entier à achever au maximum la croissance et le développement individuels et à se consacrer au service de l'humanité tout entière ». Nous pourrions, me semble-t-il, considérer ces lignes comme une déclaration de principe fournissant un préambule général à vos recommandations d'un ordre plus spécifique.

La requête la plus fréquente – six sur vingt-cinq – concerne l'éducation à la vie familiale. Cela ne s'adresse pas uniquement au système scolaire, mais dans plusieurs recommandations on estime qu'il faudrait augmenter la part donnée à l'éducation à la vie familiale dans les écoles, que cela serait possible si les professeurs y étaient mieux préparés. Quatre des groupes ont remarqué qu'ils souhaitaient que les programmes fassent une plus grande place à la créativité, ce qui a un peu troublé ce comité. Nous nous sommes demandé si, plutôt que d'insister sur le programme, on ne réclamait pas un milieu scolaire dans lequel l'écolier, pris individuellement, et ses capacités seraient identifiables et identifiés, et dans lequel on insisterait sur des professeurs imaginatifs qui abordent leur tâche avec plus de souplesse.

Quatre groupes ont recommandé que la formation des professeurs leur permette de mieux comprendre les problèmes du développement de l'enfant et de mieux identifier les déviations à la normale. Cela a été exprimé spécifiquement dans ces quatre recommandations et implicitement dans un certain nombre d'autres. Deux groupes ont insisté sur la nécessité d'une plus grande égalité dans les possibilités offertes aux enfants dans les diverses écoles, et bien que l'essentiel de la discussion concerne l'école rurale et l'école urbaine, on n'oublie pas les écoles dans les quartiers misérables. On s'est également penché sur le difficile problème de subvenir aux besoins des enfants indiens et esquimaux. Deux groupes ont étudié l'orientation à l'école. Ils ont demandé des modifications à la formation des orienteurs, afin de leur permettre davantage de compréhension et d'efficacité dans leurs services.

Plusieurs groupes ont recommandé que davantage de services consacrés à l'enfance soient rattachés à l'école. Qu'il existe davantage de services de dépistage pour dépister les petites anomalies physiques, mentales et affectives. Cela semble une idée fort sensible. Il n'y a aucune occasion, avant que l'enfant ne soit d'âge scolaire, pour l'évaluer en comparaison avec ses pairs ; par conséquent, les chances de remarquer toutes les déviations augmentent grandement quand l'enfant arrive à l'école. C'est pourquoi on a estimé important d'essayer d'encourager le développement des groupes professionnels autour du système scolaire pour qu'une fois les anomalies détectées, les services professionnels puissent agir aussitôt.

Et là, nous revenons à la recommandation que vous avez fermement exprimée, que les professionnels forment un groupe multi-disciplines. Sûrement le pivot logique en est l'école. Cela permet à leurs capacités professionnelles de venir au secours des enfants et des problèmes qui surgissent parmi eux. Nous parlons de ces problèmes comme s'il s'agissait toujours de défauts chez ces enfants qu'on dit « pas comme les autres ». Mais il est tout aussi important de reconnaître très tôt l'enfant exceptionnellement doué et de le placer dans un contexte où il pourra user de ses facultés. Voilà pourquoi nous estimons que l'école est le centre logique de ces groupes multi-disciplines.

Un des groupes a formulé une recommandation intéressante : qu'il y ait une part plus grande faite aux connaissances internationales, surtout à l'école primaire. Les délégués estiment que les enfants canadiens doivent prendre conscience de leur identité au milieu des enfants du monde, et que le sentiment d'identité nationale qui est tellement souhaitable pour nos enfants serait plus facile à atteindre si nous leur parlions davantage des enfants des autres parties du monde. Le comité estime que c'est là une recommandation pleine d'imagination.

Il y a eu un groupe – et je suis étonné qu'il n'y en ait eu qu'un seul – qui a insisté sur la nécessité, pour les professionnels, de continuer sans cesse leur éducation. Dans ma propre profession, voilà déjà quelque temps qu'on en est fortement conscient, et on a dit qu'un médecin était un peu moins efficace chaque matin, au réveil, à cause des progrès faits par la médecine pendant qu'il dormait.

L'Organisation mondiale de la santé a publié récemment quelques chiffres surprenants. Il existe aujourd'hui plus de 50,000 revues médicales dans le monde, qui publient plus de 1,200,000 articles par an, soit un nouvel article médical toutes les 23 secondes ! Voilà pourquoi le prolongement de l'éducation médicale est tellement important, au point que les douze écoles de médecine du Canada l'ont reconnu comme une de leurs responsabilités essentielles, au même titre que la formation des étudiants. Et je suppose que ce besoin va augmenter de façon visible dans les autres professions. Ce qui s'est passé, en médecine, c'est que nous avons pu obtenir des fonds pour des travaux de recherche, et ce sont ces grands travaux, prenant tant d'importance au cours des vingt dernières années, qui ont créé toute ces informations nouvelles. Que des ressources similaires soient mises au service des sciences sociales, et l'avancement se fera de façon tellement rapide que le prolongement de l'éducation deviendra nécessaire pour tous, me semble-t-il.

Le troisième secteur de préoccupations presque unanimes est celui du bénévolat. Vingt-trois sur vingt-cinq des groupes ont recommandé qu'on fasse meilleur usage des services des bénévoles. On insiste qu'en plus de former un supplément d'aide très nécessaire, cela peut fournir un centre d'intérêt à des gens qui en manquent.

On estime qu'il faut réétudier très soigneusement l'utilisation des bénévoles et y consacrer davantage d'imagination. Bien qu'on ait fréquemment mentionné la femme dont les enfants ont grandi, surtout celle qui a reçu une instruction poussée, il est étonnant de voir que vous avez surtout parlé d'utiliser les services de la jeunesse. Bien entendu, cela permet de faire d'une pierre deux coups : les adolescents les plus âgés prennent part à la tâche, et, en même temps qu'ils contribuent de leurs services, ils apprennent ce qu'est la vie en famille.

La plupart des vingt-trois recommandations émises sur le sujet font remarquer que le mot « bénévole » sert à désigner toute une variété de travailleurs, par exemple des individus dont la formation est relativement poussée aussi bien que d'autres qui n'en ont aucune, des travailleurs à plein temps qui sont rémunérés en tout ou en partie, des travailleurs à temps partiel qui ne le sont pas du tout. Ce que nous a dit Sam Rabinovitch l'autre jour sur la source de personnel qui apparaîtra le jour où l'automation raccourcira la semaine et la journée de travail se retrouve dans une ou deux de vos recommandations. Par conséquent, l'emploi intensif des bénévoles représente le troisième secteur presque unanime de vos recommandations de groupes.

L' unanimité des opinions dans ces trois domaines nous a réellement paru frappante. Mais elle s'est arrêtée là. Les autres recommandations varient d'un groupe à l'autre. Pour vous en donner une idée : cinq groupes se sont préoccupés du problème de la communication entre générations, et ces mêmes groupes ont insisté qu'il y aurait dû y avoir davantage de jeunes adultes et adolescents au nombre des délégués à ce congrès.

Au chapitre des communications, il y a également un certain nombre de groupes qui ont rattaché notre échec dans le domaine de l'éducation des parents à l'emploi insuffisant des média de masse. Ils estiment qu'on pourrait se servir de la radio et de la télévision de façon beaucoup plus efficace. Nous nous sommes posé la question : dans quelle mesure y-a-t-il éducation quand il n'y a pas participation ?

On a également parlé de la régulation des naissances et cinq groupes ont précisément réclamé que la section 150 du code soit revisée pour que soit permise la libre diffusion des informations et techniques anticonceptionnelles.

Beaucoup d'entre vous se préoccupent de la recherche. Douze groupes en tout ont abordé le problème d'une façon ou d'une autre. Six des groupes ont simplement mentionné le besoin de davantage de travaux de recherche. Deux groupes ont mentionné spécifiquement les besoins dans le domaine du foyer et de la famille, sur les plans psychologique et social. Deux autres groupes ont parlé d'enfance et surtout de jeunesse, et deux groupes estiment que l'éducation, prise comme un tout, nécessite beaucoup plus de recherches qu'on n'en a effectué jusqu'à présent. Par conséquent, la moitié de nos groupes se soucient suffisamment d'une intensification de la recherche pour mentionner spécifiquement la nécessité de consacrer des efforts à cette fin.

Vous vous êtes trouvés aux prises avec le problème du sens des valeurs, tout comme le comité des conclusions. Deux groupes insistent pour que les droits des enfants aient priorité sur les droits des parents. Et deux groupes ont recommandé l'établissement d'un sous-comité pour étudier et mettre au point une déclaration sur le sens des valeurs chez les enfants.

Vous avez longuement considéré le prochain congrès, avec sept recommandations réclamant spécifiquement un autre congrès, dont trois insistent qu'il devrait avoir lieu dans deux ans. Six suggèrent qu'il y ait des congrès et des réalisations sur le plan provincial dans l'intervalle. Trois ont suggéré que les provinces commencent à travailler à l'établissement d'une charte de l'enfance, projet sur lequel on pourrait commencer à travailler dès maintenant et qui serait accepté à ce moment-là. Trois ont insisté à nouveau pour que des jeunes soient invités à participer au prochain congrès.

Un certain nombre de groupes sont troublés par la similitude des buts de l'Institut Vanier de la famille et la Conférence canadienne de l'enfance. Cinq groupes ont spécifiquement demandé qu'on étudie et qu'on effectue si possible la fusion des groupes ou qu'on en arrive à une collaboration très étroite.

Deux groupes souhaitent que la Conférence canadienne de l'enfance organise un secrétariat permanent pour encourager l'action aux niveaux gouvernemental et local, et pour encourager la recherche dans divers domaines.

En bref, vous avez passé en revue tous les aspects et problèmes de la maturité. Vous avez identifié les obstacles et émis de sages et constructives recommandations pour les éliminer. Ce qui nous a le plus surpris, c'est l'unanimité de vos préoccupations et votre identification des trois grands domaines : communication interprofessionnelle, réévaluation de l'éducation, emploi intensifié des bénévoles. Je sais que je me fais l'interprète des organisateurs du congrès en vous disant combien nous sommes reconnaissants de l'intérêt, de l'énergie et de la sagesse dont vous avez fait preuve au cours de ces trois jours.

Si ces pages sont avant tout le rapport du comité des conclusions, elles devraient aussi dans une certaine mesure refléter le congrès, et là, elles échouent misérablement ! Comment vous retransmettre dès maintenant tout ce qui l'a composé : la profondeur des propos tenus par le Dr Myrdal le samedi soir, les déclarations franches et simples du Dr Ross, lundi matin, le brillant commentaire que nous a donné quotidiennement le Dr Thomas, et les directives passionnantes suggérées par le Dr Sam Rabinovitch et le Professeur Charles Hendry. Tout cela restera dans notre mémoire.

Au moment où le congrès s'achève, il ne faut pas oublier la somme fantastique de travail accompli par les groupes inter-disciplines au niveaux local et provincial, pour s'y préparer. Dans un sens, le congrès n'est qu'une fenêtre qui nous permet de nous rendre compte de ce qui s'est fait dans les provinces et localement, et certains des résultats de ce travail. C'est cet effort soutenu qui va, j'en suis sûr, continuer de changer l'attitude, envers les enfants, des professionnels et des autres. J'espère que, tout comme moi, vous êtes fiers d'avoir pris part au second Congrès de la conférence canadienne de l'enfance.

Humaniser ou homogénéiser?

LE TRÈS RÉVÉREND ROGER GUINDON, O.M.I.

WITHOUT UNDUE MODESTY, I confess that I am a little surprised at finding myself speaking to this learned gathering. True, your president, Mrs. Reva Gerstein, and I had become acquainted with each other when, with her colleagues on the Ontario Advisory Committee on University Affairs, she had me squirming on the grill as we discussed the budget of the University of Ottawa, over whose destiny I have the honour to preside. It would be flattering to me if I could believe that I was, at that time, weighed in the balance of her judgment and found not to be unworthy of this occasion.

I suspect, however, that I am here less in my personal right than as the head of the institution which, alone among the institutions of higher learning, is the bearer of a century-old tradition of a certain Canadianism that is, only now, stirring up a more than platonic interest across our fair country. And it is likely that it was this consideration, more than any other, which motivated the invitation that has brought me here today. Now, this concept of what I believe to be the genuine Canadianism consists essentially of a search after mutual understanding through the meeting together and cross-fertilization of our two great cultures . . . with a further enrichment from the other cultures that mingle in the Canadian society.

However, let us not be deceived. Like the word "culture" itself, the expression "cross-fertilization" is a figure of speech drawn from the field of husbandry. But the analogy is not perfect. In husbandry, the subjects of cross-fertilization are purely passive, the failure of any experiment is of little consequence and the scientist proceeds on the principle "if at first you don't succeed, try, try again." But, in Canada, the process of human cultural cross-fertilization must not fail; for there will not be a second chance. For this reason, the enlightened elements of the two cultural groups must make a positive effort at mutual understanding and especially, on the occasion of conferences such as this, they must not be content to show a polite, passive tolerance of each other's views while inwardly basking in the exclusive rightness of their own.

I can conceive of no meeting ground that demands this kind of empathy with greater urgency than a conference to study the ways and means of preparing the children of today for the Canadian society of tomorrow. For, indeed, if we are divided in many ways with respect to our constitutional and economic collective life, none of these differences presents insurmountable obstacles to our working together for the progress and prosperity of Canada. A little goodwill and a sincere spirit of compromise will, as in all democratic countries, readily adjust these differences. But in the matter of the education of children and the training of youth and of the specific part played by society therein, the problem is too deeply rooted in the basic philosophy of life to be an object of compromise, except in its more superficial aspects. If divergences exist, they cannot be composed in a sterile syncretism that sinks the differences out of sight but only in a kind of symbiosis of the best features of each.

In regard to the educational problem, I shall not say that there are two clear-cut, fixed, and irreconcilable attitudes. But, in Canada, as in most countries of the world, I can discern two tendencies that do not, by any means, coincide with any ethnic cleavage. Each may be summed up in a word: *humanize . . . homogenize.*

Ces deux mots, *humaniser* et *homogénéiser*, dont le premier remonte à plusieurs siècles et le second est de formation relativement récente, comportent tous deux la terminaison *-iser* qui implique une action transitive, un agir intentionnel sur quelqu'un ou quelque chose en vue de les transformer. Par là, ils visent la société d'aujourd'hui, fixant les yeux, comme vous l'avez fait, sur la société de demain. Or, malgré leur similarité phonétique, les racines *homo* de ces termes révèlent des contenus très différents : *humaniser*, c'est rendre plus foncièrement humain; *homogénéiser*, rendre plus complètement semblables.

Le second de ces termes décrit très bien le procédé par lequel toutes les particules du lait sont réduites à une telle identité de texture que la crème ne remonte plus à la surface. Transposée au domaine social, cette expression signifierait que l'éducation aurait pour but l'étouffement de l'élite dans la communauté, ce qui est un malheur pour une société.

Loin de moi, mesdames et messieurs, la pensée qu'il se trouverait parmi vous quelqu'un qui souhaitât à la société canadienne un tel nivellement par le bas. Mais l'esprit humain est tellement épris de l'ordre admirable qui régit la nature et du déterminisme sur lequel se fondent toutes ses sciences qu'il peut perdre de vue les caractères distinctifs de la personnalité humaine et être entraîné, inconsciemment, à confondre l'homme lui-même dans l'homogénéité universelle. Devenu ingénieur des choses, l'homme est tenté d'assurer le rôle d'ingénieur des hommes.

L'homme n'a-t-il pas en lui et autour de lui un réseau serré de déterminismes semblables à ceux qui enchaînent les autres êtres aux cycles réguliers qui les caractérisent ? L'auteur sacré, dans un langage imagé plein de signification, nous raconte que « Yahvé Dieu modela l'homme avec la glaise du sol ». Cette humble origine de l'homme est passée dans notre vocabulaire occidental si profondément marqué par l'influence chrétienne. C'est de l'*humus* que surgit l'*humanité*. Mais il n'y a pas que de la glaise dans notre blason ! La Bible ajoute en effet que Dieu « insuffla dans ses narines une haleine de vie et l'homme devint un être vivant ». Voilà vraiment la noblesse et la distinction de l'homme entre toutes les créatures : il a été fait à l'image et à la ressemblance de Dieu pour qu'il devienne maître de l'univers et de lui-même, après Dieu.

Les cycles de l'histoire de l'humanité et des hommes qui la composent sont loin d'avoir l'homogénéité qu'on retrouve ailleurs dans l'univers.

It is this homogeneity of nature that has made possible the scientific achievements of which man may justly be proud, and that opens up to our fascinated mind new boundless vistas of greater biological and technological advances. No wonder, then, that some dream of a society where man himself could be engineered into the same kind of homegeneity that enables the scientist to set the conditions and forecast the direction of biological growth and the end result of laboratory experiments. In other words, what a perfect social order we could realize if we could accept at its face value and quite literally Milton's poetic view that

> The childhood shows the man
> As morning shows the day.
> (*Paradise Regained*)

The radical difficulty is that it is simply not so. In all that makes him specifically human, man escapes from this otherwise universal homogeneity. In contrast to the breeder of sheep with a new-born lamb, the mother, fondly holding her new-born child, will always wonder what kind of adult it will grow up to be.

Science will never change this uncertainty of the human condition. All that the ever-growing number of disciplines—that we lump together under the name of "human sciences"—can hope to achieve is to improve the state of things in which the child can mature in his own way, through his own personal powers, into an adult who is respectful of the social order because society itself respects the individual personality of its members.

Am I wrong in saying that—in sharp contrast with what takes place in a totalitarian state—the aim of a democratic educational system is to assist in the fullest possible development of the human personality rather than to shape all personalities in the same mould? Yet, in no other sphere of human activity has the movement toward socialization been as extensive as in the field of education. I am not referring to the financial and organizational aspects of our educational system where socialization was as inevitable as it was desirable; but to its formal, fundamental element which is the intellectual, moral, and cultural unfolding of the child's personality.

« Le cerveau d'un enfant » écrit Plutarque, « n'est pas un vase qu'il faut remplir, mais un foyer qu'il faut activer ». Vraiment, s'il ne s'agissait que de remplir de jeunes cerveaux, l'accumulation prodigieuse du savoir ne nous laisserait plus qu'un choix déconcertant ! Mais à quoi cela peut-il servir au citoyen de demain si ces abondantes connaissances ne deviennent pas la matière d'où peut jaillir une pensée sainement rationnelle ? Seule la raison – par opposition à des réactions purement émotives – rend le dialogue possible et le dialogue est la condition nécessaire de la bonne marche d'une démocratie.

Le temps et peut-être votre patience, mesdames et messieurs, ne me permettent pas un examen détaillé de la formation vraiment intellectuelle que reçoivent nos jeunes sur les bancs de l'école. Ne puis-je pas, cependant, rappeler qu'une foule d'indices, à la portée quotidienne de chacun, tend à montrer que notre génération – et même un bon nombre de ses « intellectuels » – réagit avec plus d'émotivité que de raison aux événements de la vie ? Si ces signes sont révélateurs, je me crois en droit de proposer que nos dirigeants, à tous les paliers du système scolaire, se penchent davantage sur le problème de la maturation intellectuelle des jeunes.

I should not be accused of disparaging the incalculable contribution made by the scientists, the industrialists, and the artists to human welfare, if I say that—more than all these advantages—society, any society, needs members of staunch moral calibre if it is not to become, in the words of Saint Augustine, merely "a den of thieves." Society was always able to do without a better mouse-trap and, strictly speaking, it can still do without more perfect computers and speedier means of communications. But no society can long endure if its members in the aggregate are not possessed of solid moral convictions.

I am not among the prophets of doom who believe that morality has completely crumbled in our society. However—like most of you, I am sure—I cannot completely shake off a certain feeling of uneasiness at the present-day developments in our personal and social behaviour.

Emotions and feelings cannot constitute a valid norm of ethical conduct. They are too closely linked to the "here and now," to concrete circumstances and the protean whims and fancies of the individual; and their normative validity is not increased amply through being shared, at a given moment, by any number of other individuals. Morality can have only one basis, and that is an intellectual principle, or set of principles, that transcends the individual and the changing conditions of everyday life.

Now, no society in the past has found—and I, personally, venture to say: no society in the future will find—a substitute for religion as the transcendental basis of morality. Religious belief does assume a variety of forms, but always it should be nurtured in the minds and hearts of the growing generations as an authentic and indispensable human value, because it can sate the hunger of man for "the absolute."

In many regions of the Western world, society has shrugged off all interest in this human value, so far as its public school system is concerned. Or religion has been diluted so thinly that it has lost all its effectiveness. We have passed the stage where a society attempts forcibly to cast its members in the same religious mould. Conveniently forgetting that the intolerance of the past and the bitter reactions it provoked were, nevertheless, a vivid acknowledgement of the human value of religion, we now boast of official tolerance which, in point of fact, is nothing more than a complete surrender in the face of a thorny practical problem, the problem of diversity. There is here no intention to homogenize, but the end-result is the same: a depreciation of society through the gradual suppression of the most effective rule of morality.

Alors que la majorité des Canadiens grandissent dans un système scolaire que j'appellerai, en gros, « a-religieux », ils subissent l'influence d'un système « mono-culturel ». Cette dimension humaine ne possède pas une importance aussi essentielle que la première, mais elle comporte un élément de telle nature que les tendances homogénéisantes et humanisantes s'y heurtent avec plus d'éclat. Du reste, cette politique de mono-culturalisme se comprend aisément si on la situe dans le cadre d'une certaine philosophie qui voit la réalisation parfaite du bien commun dans l'établissement de l'uniformité d'où les particularismes sont exclus. Dans un état totalitaire, ces particularismes sont impitoyablement étouffés ; dans une démocratie évoluée, on les considère comme un mal nécessaire, l'objet de mesquines concessions pour l'amour de l'ordre et de la paix.

Il est pourtant une autre idée du bien commun selon laquelle les particularismes sont dignes du plus grand respect. Non seulement le pouvoir politique n'y porte pas atteinte, mais il les protège, les entretient, un peu comme le jardinier qui porte une égale attention à chacune des fleurs variées de ses plates-bandes, ou comme le chef d'orchestre qui voit dans la diversité des instruments une sorte de défi à son génie musical. Ainsi dans cette conception du bien commun l'ordre social ne réside pas dans l'uniformité, mais dans l'arrangement harmonieux de parties diverses agissant de concert pour le plus grand bien de l'ensemble.

Mesdames et messieurs, dans tous les pays où l'histoire l'a instauré, le bilinguisme a toujours soulevé des problèmes tant pour la majorité que pour les pouvoirs publics. Le généraliser à tous les paliers du système scolaire canadien entraînerait des mises de fonds considérables et des complications fastidieuses. Certains prétendent même qu'il priverait l'école d'un temps mieux employé à meubler le cerveau de l'enfant de connaissances prétendues plus utiles. Nous connaissons à fond ces problèmes à l'université d'Ottawa et dans les écoles bilingues de l'Ontario et d'ailleurs. Mais nous n'avons pas accepté la solution facile qui consiste à méconnaître la valeur essentiellement humaine pour le Canada d'un bilinguisme authentique et à se laver les mains d'une situation, compliquée sans doute, mais qui n'est pas sans issue. Nous n'avons certes pas atteint l'idéal. Nous y travaillons !

On behalf of the French Canadians, I wholeheartedly acknowledge the generous efforts made by a large number of our English-speaking compatriots to learn French. And my special felicitations go to those who are inspired not by fear or a narrow self-interest, but by the recognition that the course of history has made of French a valuable asset in Canada and that, if our country is to be united in a common vision of greatness, communications among its citizens cannot indefinitely remain a one-way street.

As in the religious and intellectual fields, the direction of our cultural growth is ours to decide. Should the Canadian society be more intensively humanized by the promotion of diversity in unity or should it be more thoroughly homogenized through the reduction of diversity to uniformity? There is here more than "a distinction without a difference."

Ladies and gentlemen, it was asked of me that my remarks on this occasion be provocative of reflection. In this short talk on a subject of such scope and consequence, I could not avoid over-generalizations and over-simplifications. I am fully conscious of them, but precisely, the necessity of making the proper distinction and deciding the practically possible course that our society should adopt in the interests of a greater Canada, should provide ample food for thought.

Quelles que soient les réactions qu'aient du provoquer en vous les idées que j'ai émises ici, je tiens à déclarer en terminant que je n'ai eu d'autre intention que de développer dans toutes l'ampleur qu'elle me semble posséder, l'idée si féconde exprimée dans l'introduction du rapport Bladen sur *Le financement de l'enseignement supérieur au Canada* – et je cite :

> Gardons-nous de l'idée totalitaire qui consiste à traiter les hommes comme des moyens à développer selon les besoins de la collectivité ; considérons au contraire la collectivité comme un moyen de développer les talents des individus. A la longue, il se pourrait même que nous obtenions des revenus plus élevés en accordant une plus grande attention à l'individu. Nous serions alors sûrement plus près de réaliser une certaine plénitude de vie.

Epilogue

The Canadian Conference on Children has taken its place as an important part of the Canadian tradition. The 1965 Conference enhanced and reinforced the spirit of dedication born in 1960. We came away more convinced than ever that through partnership and mutual understanding between those persons concerned with the well-being of children, giant strides can be taken. There emerged a new commitment to continuing communication between the professions and a new faith in professional and volunteer partnership on behalf of children.

In order to reflect the continuing nature of its organization and to allow for the implementation of its aim, the Conference decided to become the Canadian Council on Children and Youth with a permanent office and secretariat. To study and implement the conclusions of this Conference and to prepare for the next, the provincial committees will be increasingly active. There is much to be accomplished but we will move forward with confidence, secure in the knowledge that all across Canada there are people dedicated to the aims for which we stand.

In 1957 we chose as our symbol two children superimposed on the background of Canada. Now, somehow, they seem to be taller, and are smiling as they are marching on the "Road to Maturity."

Epilogue

La Conférence canadienne de l'enfance a maintenant une place importante dans la tradition canadienne. Le congrès de 1965 n'a fait que donner plus d'essor au mouvement et à l'esprit nés en 1960. Nous sommes plus convaincus que jamais, que, grâce à l'association et à la compréhension mutuelle de tous ceux qui se consacrent au bien-être de l'enfance, il sera possible d'avancer à pas de géants.

Afin de mieux refléter la permanence de l'organisation et lui permettre de réaliser ses buts, la conférence à décidé de devenir le Conseil canadien de l'enfance et de le jeunesse, avec un bureau et un secrétariat permanent. Pour étudier et traduire en actions les conclusions du congrès, et pour préparer le prochain, les comités provinciaux vont connaître de plus en plus d'activité. Il y a beaucoup à faire mais nous arriverons, et nous avançons avec confiance, parce que nous savons que dans le pays tout entier il y a des gens qui se consacrent aux buts qui sont les nôtres.

En 1957, nous avons choisi comme symbole deux enfants se profilant sur la carte du Canada. Aujourd'hui, il me semble qu'ils ont grandi et qu'ils sourient, en s'avançant vers la maturité.

APPENDIXES

APPENDICES

PREPARATORY DOCUMENTS* /

DOCUMENTS PRÉPARATOIRES†

The Social Bases of Education / Les bases sociales de l'education, Frank E. Jones, Ph.D.

The Social Behaviour Surrounding Children's Health Problems / Les conduites sociales relatives aux problèmes de la santé publique, Silvia Lamb, M.A., and David N. Solomon, Ph.D.

The Social Bases of Maturity in Childhood / Les fondements sociaux de la maturation chez l'enfant, Marc-Adelard Tremblay, Ph.D.

Child Welfare Services: Winding Paths to Maturity / Service social à l'enfance: chemins sinueux à la maturation, E. Ray Godfrey, M.A., and Benjamin Schlesinger, Ph.D.

*A limited supply of copies of these documents are available at $2.00 each from: Canadian Council on Children and Youth; 165 Bloor Street East, Suite 302; Toronto 5, Ontario

†On peut se procurer un nombre limité de copies de ces documents à $2.00 chacune à: Canadian Council on Children and Youth; 165 Bloor Street East, Suite 302; Toronto 5, Ontario

BOARD OF DIRECTORS / LE CONSEIL D'ADMINISTRATION

Finance Committee / Comité du finance

St. Clair Balfour, Chairman, Toronto
Edson Boyd, Winnipeg
Ubald Boyer, Montréal
Harvey Cruickshank, m.d., Montréal
Louis Desrochers, Edmonton
Robert S. Grant, m.d., Halifax
David Sinclair, Vancouver

CONFERENCE COMMITTEES / COMITÉS DE LA CONFÉRENCE

Conclusions Committee / Comité des conclusions

Dr. J. F. McCreary, Chairman
Dr. K. S. Armstrong, Dr. Reva Gerstein, Professor C. E. Hendry, Dr. M. S. Rabinovitch, Dr. Alan Ross, Mrs. J. D. Taylor, Dr. Alan Thomas

Steering Committee / Comité d'orientation de la conférence

Mrs. W. H. Sparrow, Chairman
Mrs. J. G. Bishop, Miss Eleanor J. Bradley, Mrs. T. H. Dunn, Mme. P. Tascherau, M. Clément Thibert, Dr. Morgan Wright

Public Relations Committee / Comité des relations extérieures

Miss Rosemary Dudley, Toronto; Mrs. Lynne MacFarlane, Winnipeg; Mrs. Phyllis L. Peterson, Montréal; Mlle Henriette Robaday, Montréal; Mrs. Grace Shaw, Vancouver

Conference Staff / Personnel de la conférence

Executive Secretary: Dr. Margery R. King
Information Officer: Miss Pat Harrison
Secretary: Miss Velma Faulkner

DISCUSSION GROUP LEADERS / CHEFS DE GROUPES

RICHARD D. MCDONALD, Co-ordinator of Discussion Group Program, Sir George Williams University, Montréal

Mme C. BABIN-MICHON, c.s.p., Hôpital Sacré-Cœur pour épileptiques, Québec

F. G. BARRETT, Director of Rehabilitation, Nova Scotia Sanitarium, Kentville

Mme RITA CADIEUX, Ministère de la citoyenneté et de l'immigration, Montréal

FRED CALOREN, Associate Secretary, Student Christian Movement, Toronto

R. A. CRAIG, Consultant in Social Work, Mental Health Division, Department of National Health and Welfare, Ottawa

Mrs. MURIEL DUCKWORTH, Adult Education Division, Department of Education, Halifax

GLEN A. EYFORD, Assistant Director, Extension Department, University of Alberta, Edmonton

Miss ANNE FURNESS, Associate Professor, School of Social Work, University of British Columbia, Vancouver

Mme SUZEL PERRON, Association canadienne pour la santé mentale, Montréal

Dr. ELIZABETH HILLMAN, Director, Out-patient Department, Montreal Children's Hospital

Professor MYER KATZ, Director, School of Social Work, McGill University, Montréal

Mrs. AGNES JOHNSTON, Social Service Department, Montreal Children's Hospital

Dr. C. LABERGE-NADEAU, Hôpital Sainte-Justine, Montréal

Dr. JEAN LOUIS LAPOINTE, Directeur médical, Hôpital Mont-Providence, Montréal

Miss JOSEPHINE LYNAM, Citizenship Branch, Department of Citizenship and Immigration, Ottawa

BRUCE MACFARLAND, Verdun-Lasalle YMCA, Verdun

Miss MARJORIE SMITH, Extension Department, University of British Columbia, Vancouver

Sœur PIERRE DU CHRIST, Clairséjour, Montréal

ROGER PRUD'HOMME, Directeur de la Société de service social aux familles, Montréal

Father ANDRÉ RENAUD, Associate Professor of Education, University of Saskatchewan, Saskatoon

ROBERT R. ROBINSON, Director of Education, Alcoholism and Drug Addiction Research Foundation, Toronto

ROBERT R. ROSS, Supervising Psychologist, Training School for Boys, Cobourg

ALEX SIM, Strathmere Associates, North Gower

Mrs. MARION WALSH, Family Life Education Council, Montréal

Mrs. RUNA WOOLGAR, Family Life Education Council, Montréal

DELEGATES / DÉLÉGUÉS

International Delegates / Délégués internationaux

Professor S. C. Best, Associate Professor, Maternal and Child Health, School of Public Health, University of Michigan, Ann Arbor, Michigan
Dr. Eli Bower, Consultant, Mental Health in Education, National Institute of Mental Health, Bethesda, Maryland
Donald Dowling, Child Welfare League of America, New York
Dr. Amy Hostler, President, Mills College, New York
Dr. Helen K. Mackintosh, Elementary Schools Section, United States Office of Education, Washington, D.C.
Her Excellency Dr. Alva Myrdal, Ministry of Foreign Affairs, Sweden (Ambassador on special assignment to the United Nations)
Miss Jean Reynolds, Children's Bureau, Department of Health, Education and Welfare, Washington, D.C.

General Canadian Delegates / Délégués généraux de Canada

Dr. K. S. Armstrong, Executive Director, Canadian Rehabilitation Council for the Disabled, Toronto
St. Clair Balfour, National Film Board, Montréal
J-M. Beauchemin, Secrétaire général, Fédération des collèges classiques, Montréal
Mme Marie Blais-Grenier, Département de Sociologique, Université Laval, Québec
Mrs. J. H. Bredin, Director, Child Study Centre, University of British Columbia, Vancouver
J. A. Carmichael, Director of Rehabilitation Services, Society for Crippled Children and Adults, Winnipeg
Miss Jean Carmichael, Assistant Director, Fitness and Amateur Sport Programme, Department of National Health and Welfare, Ottawa
Miss Elspeth Chisholm, Research Director, National Film Board, Montréal
Mr. R. A. Craig, Consultant in Social Work, Mental Health Division, Department of National Health and Welfare, Ottawa
Miss Jean Dorgan, Co-ordinator of Vocational Rehabilitation Services, Civilian Rehabilitation Branch, Department of Labour, Ottawa
Mrs. T. H. Dunn, Chairman, Local Arrangements Committee, Sillery, P.Q.
Dr. J. H. Ebbs, Hospital for Sick Children, Toronto
Dr. Reva Gerstein, President, Canadian Conference on Children, Don Mills
Stewart Goodings, Assistant Secretary, Organizing Committee, Company of Young Canadians, Toronto

The Honourable Allan Grossman, Minister of Reform Institutions, Province of Ontario, Toronto
Le très révérend Roger Guindon, o.m.i., Recteur, Université d'Ottawa
Mrs. H. P. Hill, Canadian Government Participation, Expo 1967, Ottawa
Dr. Frank E. Jones, Department of Sociology, McMaster University, Hamilton
C. N. Knight, Principal Welfare Grants Officer, Department of National Health and Welfare, Ottawa
The Honourable Judy LaMarsh, Minister of National Health and Welfare, Ottawa
Miss Josephine Lynam, Liaison Officer, Citizenship Branch, Department of Citizenship and Immigration, Ottawa
Colin MacAndrew, National School Broadcasts and Youth Programming, Canadian Broadcasting Corporation, Toronto
Mrs. Lynne MacFarlane, Public Relations, Winnipeg
Dr. J. F. McCreary, Dean of Medicine, University of British Columbia, Vancouver
F. S. Neville, Division of Welfare, Department of Northern Affairs and National Resources, Ottawa
Michael Palko, Health Education Consultant, Department of National Health and Welfare, Ottawa
R. H. Parkinson, Assistant National Director of Family Allowances, Department of National Health and Welfare, Ottawa
Miss Margaret Payne, Head, Welfare Services Section, Indian Affairs Branch, Department of Citizenship and Immigration, Ottawa
Mrs. Phyllis Peterson, Information Officer, Montreal Children's Hospital, Montréal
Dr. M. S. Rabinovitch, Stillman Memorial Research Scientist, McGill University, Montréal
Dr. Fred Rainsberry, Network Supervisor, Schools and Youth Programming, Canadian Broadcasting Corporation, Toronto
Miss Henriette Robadey, Public Relations, Montreal Trust Company
Dr. Alan Ross, Professor of Paediatrics and Director, Montreal Children's Hospital
The Honourable Dr. J. D. Ross, Minister of Health, Province of Alberta, Edmonton
Mrs. Grace Shaw, Public Relations, Vancouver
Eric Smit, Consultant on Family and Child Welfare, Department of National Health and Welfare, Ottawa
Dr. David N. Solomon, Department of Sociology and Anthropology, McGill University, Montréal
Mrs. W. H. Sparrow, Executive Secretary, Cerebral Palsy Association of Québec, Montréal
Mme Pierre Taschereau, Co-ordinator of Volunteers, Montréal
Mrs. J. D. Taylor, Chairman of Nominating Committee, Canadian Conference on Children, Hamilton
Dr. Alan Thomas, Director, Canadian Association for Adult Education, Toronto
Dr Marc-Adélard Tremblay, Département de Sociologie, Université Laval, Québec

MICHEL TROTTIER, Département de Sociologie, Université Laval, Québec
Mrs. JOYCE WAITE, Education Consultant, Metropolitan Toronto Branch, Canadian Mental Health Association
Dr. JEAN F. WEBB, Chief, Maternal and Child Health Division, Department of National Health and Welfare, Ottawa
Dr. J. W. WILLARD, Deputy Minister of Welfare, Department of National Health and Welfare, Ottawa

Alberta Delegates / Délégués de l'Alberta

The Rev. P. B. O'BYRNE, Provincial Co-Chairman, Director, Catholic Charities, Calgary
Dr. STANLEY C. CLARKE, Provincial Co-Chairman, Director, Alberta Teachers' Federation, Edmonton
The Rev. RUSSELL BEARISTO, Southminster United Church, Calgary
Dr. STANLEY S. BLANK, Department of Educational Psychology, University of Alberta, Calgary
DR. T. C. BYRNE, Deputy Minister, Department of Education, Edmonton
Mrs. BERYL EBERTS, Nursing Consultant, Maternal and Child Health, Department of Public Health, Edmonton
Mr. W. A. FLETCHER, Edmonton Family Service Association, Edmonton
Mrs. A. GARBUTT, Past President, Alberta Home and School Association, Calgary
Dr. METRO GULUTZAN, Assistant Professor of Educational Psychology, University of Alberta, Edmonton
Dr. ELIZABETH HILL, Director, Sturgeon Health Unit, St. Albert
A. E. HOHOL, Assistant Superintendent, Edmonton Public School Board
Dr. ROBERT LAWSON, Acting Head, Department of Educational Foundations, University of Alberta, Calgary
Miss FLORENCE MACDONALD, Visiting Teacher, Calgary Separate School Board, Calgary
The Rev. IAN MACMILLAN, Minister, St. Paul's United Church, Edmonton
The Rev. Sister MARY CELESTINE, Social Worker, Edmonton Catholic Family Service
The Rev. Sister MARY DAMIAN, Supervisor, Providence Hospital, Grande Prairie
Mrs. ANNA PARKINSON, Alderman, Social Worker, Red Deer
F. A. SCHNEIDER, Separate School Board, Edmonton
Dr. E. S. O. SMITH, Director of Local Health Services, Alberta Department of Public Health, Edmonton
Mrs. JUNE TAYLOR, Director of Nursing Paediatrics, Royal Alexandra Hospital, Edmonton
A. H. ZIAI, Edmonton Welfare Council, Edmonton

British Columbia Delegates / Délégués de la Colombie-britannique

Miss ELEANOR J. BRADLEY, Provincial Chairman, Child Health Programme, University of British Columbia, Vancouver

Mrs. H. B. Barrett, Parent, Trail
Miss Alice Beattie, Nursing Consultant, Department of Health Services and Hospital Insurance, Victoria
T. D. Bingham, Superintendent of Child Welfare, Department of Social Welfare, Victoria
Dr. J. R. Brummitt, Director, Child Health Programme, University of British Columbia, Vancouver
Miss Lillian Carscadden, Family Service Agency, Vancouver
R. Harvey Davidson,. Supervisor, Special Education, Coquitlam
W. H. Gaddes, Professor and Head, Department of Psychology, University of Victoria
Dr. Charles Gregory, Mental Health Centre, Victoria
E. E. Hyndman, District Superintendent of Schools, Victoria
Dr. Sydney Israels, Professor and Chairman, Department of Paediatrics, University of British Columbia, Vancouver
Miss Anne Jenkins, Nursing Supervisor, Health Centre for Children, Vancouver
Dr. Andrew Mikita, Psychologist, North Shore Health Unit, North Vancouver
J. A. Mollberg, Regional Director, Department of Social Welfare, Dawson Creek
Mrs. T. L. Perry, Parent, Vancouver
J. Phillipson, Co-ordinator of Special Services, Department of Education, Victoria
S. H. Pinkerton, Children's Aid Society of Vancouver
John W. Porteous, Chairman, Greater Victoria School Board
The Rev. J. E. Reiter, Executive Director, Catholic Children's Aid Society, Vancouver
Mrs. Dorothy Rizer, Assistant Professor, College and Faculty of Education, University of British Columbia, Vancouver
Basil A. Robinson, Planning Associate, Welfare and Recreation Community Chest and councils of the Greater Vancouver Area
Miss Audrey Selander, Project Director, Area Development Project, Vancouver
Miss Marjorie V. Smith, Supervisor, Community Organization and Family Life Consultant in Adult Education, University of British Columbia, Vancouver
Mrs. H. L. Steves, Parent-Teacher Association, Richmond
The Rev. William Van Druten, Gordon United Church, Victoria
Mrs. J. W. Whitelaw, Women's Auxiliary, Health Centre for Children, Vancouver
Miss E. Williamson, Director of Nursing, Metropolitan Health Services of Greater Vancouver
Miss Jean Wilton, Special Counsellor, School District 23, Kelowna

Manitoba Delegates / Délégués de Manitoba

Dr. Morgan Wright, Provincial Chairman, Chief Psychologist Winnipeg General Hospital

Dr. J. L. Asselstine, Director, Child Guidance Clinic, Winnipeg
Mrs. A. B. Brown, Executive Director, Day Nursery Centre, Winnipeg
Mr. W. H. Bury, Executive Director, Children's Aid Society, Winnipeg
The Rev. Father Léo Couture, Parish Priest, St. Norbert
Eric E. Cox, Supervisor of Staff Training, Attorney General's Department, Winnipeg
David Critchley, Executive Director, the Children's Home of Winnipeg
Miss Mary Easterbrook, Associate Professor, School of Social Work, University of Manitoba
Miss Betty Gibson, Primary Supervisor, Brandon Elementary Schools
Bruce Fraser, Executive Director, Children's Aid Society of Central Manitoba, Portage la Prairie
H. H. Guest, Guidance Supervisor, Winnipeg School Division
Mrs. Margaret Mackling, District Director, Victorian Order of Nurses, Winnipeg
Frank Mak, Children's Aid Society of Eastern Manitoba, St. Boniface
Dr. Kenneth M. McRae, Assistant Professor of Paediatrics, Winnipeg Children's Hospital
Mrs. Howard Murphy, Manager Industrial Workshop, The Society for Crippled Children and Adults, Winnipeg
Mitchel Neiman, Secretary, Child Care and Family Division, Community Welfare Planning Council, Winnipeg
Dr. R. Parker, Director, Child Guidance Clinic, Hospital for Mental Diseases, Brandon
Dr. Ella L. Peters, Director, Department of Health, Winnipeg
Mrs. H. C. Reisberry, Executive Director, the Children's Aid Society of Western Manitoba, Brandon
Professor Douglas Rennie, Professor of Sociology, University of Manitoba, Winnipeg
Mrs. J. Marie Salway, Health Educator, Neepawa Health Unit
Judge Nellie McNichol Sanders, Winnipeg Juvenile Court and Family Court
A. D. Thomson, Assistant Superintendent, The Winnipeg School Division No. 1
Dean W. J. Waines, Vice-President, University of Manitoba, Winnipeg
James B. Waite, Regional Director, Provincial Department of Welfare, Winnipeg
Peter Wilby, Special Education, Department of Education, Winnipeg

New Brunswick Delegates / Délégués de Nouvelle Brunswick

Mrs. J. G. Bishop, Provincial Chairman, Social Worker, Saint John
Dr. A. D. Bona, Dentist, Saint John
Miss Bernadine Conlogue, Children's Aid Society, Saint John
Travis W. Cushing, Assistant Superintendent of Schools, Saint John
Miss Kathleen Donahue, Supervisor of Nurses, Saint John Board of Health
Louis J. Hachey, Youth Services Representative, Department of Youth and Welfare, Bathurst

Mrs. Eileen Higgins, Teacher, Lancaster
Dr. Roch Khazen, Director, Maternal and Child Health, Department of Health, Fredericton
Dr. R. Glen MacDonald, Chief of Staff, Children's Division, Saint John General Hospital
John MacDonald, Administrator, Moncton Family and Children's Service, Moncton
Miss Margaret MacLachlan, Associate Professor, School of Nursing, Department of Health, Fredericton
Miss Ruby MacNeill, Supervisor of Home Economics, Saint John City Schools
Miss Kathleen Morrissy, Supervisor, Welfare Services, Department of National Health and Welfare, Fredericton
Mlle Apolline Robichaud, Director, Public Health Nursing Division, Department of Health, Fredericton
Miss Thelma Sewell, Director of Home Economics, Department of Education, Fredericton
Miss Dorothy M. Sharp, District Director, Victorian Order of Nurses, Saint John
Miss Edna M. Smith, New Brunswick Protestant Orphans Home, Saint John
Stanley T. Spicer, Director of Adult Education and Physical Fitness, Department of Education, Fredericton
Dr. John Stanley, Medical Superintendent, Children's Hospital School, Lancaster

Nova Scotia Delegates / Délégués de Nouvelle Écosse

D. H. Johnson, Provincial Chairman, Director of Child Welfare, Department of Public Welfare, Halifax
Boyd B. Barteaux, Superintendent of Schools, Truro
The Rev. Colin Campbell, Diocesan Director, Catholic Charities Office, Halifax
Dr. H. B. Colford, Director, Maternal and Child Health, Department of Public Health, Halifax
Miss Marjorie A. Cook, Director of Special Services, Board of School Commissioners, Halifax
James E. Deagle, Vice-President, Nova Scotia Teachers' Union, Antigonish
Dr. F. A. Dunsworth, Associate Professor of Psychiatry, Dalhousie University, Halifax
Dr. R. S. Grant, Paediatrician, Halifax
A. W. Hendsbee, District Supervisor, Department of Welfare, Digby
Dr. Doris L. Hirsch, Psychiatrist, Halifax
Sister John Elizabeth, Superintendent, Home of the Guardian Angel, Halifax
G. W. MacKenzie, Chief Inspector of Schools, Department of Education, Halifax
Dr. Ruth McDougall, Director of Maternal and Child Health, Halifax
Sister Mary Clare, Sister Superior, Saint Joseph's Orphanage, Halifax

Dr. W. P. OLIVER, Field Representative, Adult Education Division, Department of Education, Bedford
Mrs. FREDA VICKERY, Director, Social Welfare Department, The Children's Hospital, Halifax
Dr. ULRICH A. WESTE, Paediatrician, Dartmouth

Ontario Delegates / Délégués de l'Ontario

Professor C. E. HENDRY, Provincial Chairman, Director, School of Social Work, University of Toronto
Miss DOROTHY ADAMS, Supervisor of Nurses, Public Health Unit, Fort William
Dr. JEAN ALEXANDER, Assistant Director, Child Health Program, Queen's University, Kingston
Dr. W. ARMOUR, Assistant Secretary, Ontario Medical Association, Toronto
Miss MARGARET ARMSTRONG, Student, University of Toronto
JUDGE HUGH C. ARRELL, Judge, Juvenile and Family Court, Hamilton
RAY AULD, Executive Director, Ontario Society for Crippled Children, Toronto
MISS ISABEL BLACK, Director of Public Health Nursing, Ontario Department of Health, Toronto
SID BLUM, Research Director, Hamilton Social Planning Council
Mrs. OLIVE BOLTON, Supervisor of Protection and Child Care, Children's Aid Society of Waterloo-Kitchener
RALPH S. BOOT, Police Inspector, Police Youth Bureau of Metropolitan Toronto
Mrs. JUNE BRAATEN, Co-ordinator of Recreation Services, Ontario Association for Retarded Children, Don Mills
Dr. CAROL BUCK, Professor of Preventive Medicine, University of Western Ontario, London
Miss MARGARET BURNS, Director of Casework, Toronto Mental Health Clinic
Mrs. HELEN CAVE, Social Work Supervisor, Queen's University, Kingston
Miss IMELDA CHENARD, Senior Planning Secretary, Ottawa Welfare Council
Miss BARBARA CHISHOLM, Executive Director, Victoria Day Nursery, Toronto
Mrs. CHARLES CONNOLLY, National Secretary, Christian Family Movement, Toronto
Dr. DOUGLAS CRAM, Medical Director, London Board of Education
JEROME D. DIAMOND, Executive Director, Jewish Family and Child Service, Toronto
Dr. HAROLD ELBORN, Assistant Deputy Minister of Education, Toronto
Miss BEATRICE ESSERY, Public Health Nurse, Ridgetown Office, Kent County Health Unit, Chatham
The Rev. FRANK FIDLER, Association Secretary, Board of Christian Education, United Church of Canada, Toronto
MISS JEAN FORREST, Supervisor of Public Health Nursing, Sudbury and District Health Unit
Miss MARGARET GRANT, Principal, Metropolitan Toronto School for the Deaf

Dr. Elizabeth Govan, Professor, School of Social Work, University of Toronto

Mrs. Helen M. Johnston, Alderman, City of Toronto

Mrs. Margaret Kirkpatrick, Assistant Professor, School of Social Work, University of Toronto

Mrs. Louise Lashbrook, Speech Consultant, Board of Education, London

Miss Bea Longley, Teacher, Eastdale Vocational School, Toronto

Cecil Longmuir, Principal, Givins Senior School, Toronto

Mrs. Stuart MacKay, Community Volunteer, Toronto

Ernest Majury, Manager, Family and Children's Services of Peel County, Brampton

Mrs. Freda Manson, Assistant Director, Ontario Welfare Council, Toronto

The Rev. John Albert Mattice, Parish Priest, Guelph

Gordon G. McClure, Teacher of Adjustment Class, Hawthorn School, Ottawa

Mrs. Inez McCoy, Parent, Ashton

Dr. Margaret McCready, Dean, Macdonald Institute, University of Guelph

Dr. B. H. McNeel, Director, Professional Services Branch, Mental Health Division, Ontario Department of Health, Toronto

D. S. Mewhort, Co-ordinator of Auxiliary Services, Toronto Board of Education

Mrs. Catherine Michalski, Teacher of Occupations' Class, Kingston Board of Education

Miss Dorothy Millichamp, Associate Professor and Supervisor of Academic Programme, Institute of Child Study, University of Toronto

Dr. F. A. Olivieri, Paediatrician, Hamilton

Miss Helen Palmer, Co-ordinator, Medical Nursing, Hospital for Sick Children, Toronto

Dr. Rene J. Paquin, Research Chemist, Brockville

Dr. Lyon N. Pearlman, Professor of Paediatrics, University of Ottawa

Miss Arlette Pederson, Assistant to the President, Waterloo Lutheran University

Mrs. Lavada Pinder, Supervisor of Family Services, Children's Aid Society, Kingston

Mrs. M. G. Powell, Lecturer, School of Nursing, Queen's University, Kingston

Mrs. W. F. Prendergast, Community volunteer, Toronto

Mrs. Vivian Pullan, Psychologist, Toronto

Dr. John Read, Professor and Head, Department of Preventive Medicine, Queen's University, Kingston

Mrs. J. A. Rhind, Community volunteer, Toronto

Lloyd S. Richardson, Executive Director, Childrens' Aid Society of Metropolitan Toronto

Malcolm Savage, Chief Social Worker, Children's Psychiatric Research Institute, London

Robert Shaw, Executive Director, Boy's Village, Downsview

Donald Sinclair, Executive Director, Ontario Division, Canadian Mental Health Association, Toronto

Miss Ethel Stevens, Unit Supervisor, Nursery and Day Care Services, Department of Public Welfare, Toronto
Mrs. Frances Strick, Public Health Nurse, Child Health Program, Queen's University, Kingston
Dr. L. W. Sturgeon, Medical Officer of Health, Welland County Health Unit, Welland
H. E. Thomas, Director of Youth Branch, Ontario Department of Education, Toronto
Dr. Margaret Thompson, Assistant Professor of Paediatrics, Department of Genetics, Hospital for Sick Children, Toronto
Mrs. Ruth M. F. Thompson, Librarian, Ottawa Public Library
Elmer Toffelmire, Provincial Probation Officer, Kitchener
Mrs. Vincent Voaden, Teacher, Forest Hill Village School, Toronto
R. K. Vogan, Inspector of Public Schools, Ottawa
Miss Jessie Watters, Casework Consultant, Children's Aid Society of Metropolitan Toronto
Miss Joan Wilson, Public Health Nurse, Kent County Health Unit, Chatham
Dr. M. C. A. Zurowska, National President, Canadian Polish Women's Federation, Sudbury

Prince Edward Island Delegates / Délégués de l'Ile du Prince Édouard

Russell Ewing, Provincial Chairman, Chief Psychologist, Mental Health Clinic, Charlottetown
J. E. Green, Regional Director, Family Allowances and Old Age Security, Charlottetown
Vincent E. McIntyre, Probation Supervisor, Department of Welfare and Labour, Charlottetown
Dr. Kenneth Parker, Superintendent of Schools, Charlottetown

Délégués de Québec / Quebec Delegates

Clément Thibert, Président Provincial, Directeur du Bureau de l'enfance exceptionelle, Ministère de l'Education, Québec
Mrs. D. A. Aitken, Rosemere
Dr Gérard Barbeau, Directeur général des études, Commission des écoles catholiques de Montréal
Dr Dominique Bédard, Directeur des Services psychiatriques, Ministère de la santé, Montréal
Mme M. Bédard-Delage, Montréal
M. Gabriel Blanchard, Montréal
Dr M. Blanchet-Patry, Médecin-chef, Unité sanitaire Hochelaga, Rivière-des-Prairies
Dr Marcel Boily, Directeur médical, Clinique de réadaptation pour enfants, Trois-Rivières
M. René Boisvert, Service social du diocèse d'Amos, Amos

Le rév. ROLAND BOULET, Marsboro, Co. Frontenac
Dr. HYMAN CAPLAN, Assistant Director, Department of Psychiatry, Montreal Children's Hospital
Dr RAYMOND CARON, Directeur, Manoir Charles de Foucauld, Giffard
Mrs. KAY CROWE, Director, Family Life Education Council, Montréal
Dr. RITA DAIGLE-LOCK, Pédiatre, Hôpital Ste-Justine et Hôpital Mont-Providence, Pierrefonds .
M. BERNARD DESGAGNÉ, Centre de réhabilitation, Hôtel-Dieu St-Vallier, Chicoutimi
Mlle RITA DOYON, Assistante-infirmière en chef, Département de la santé, Montréal
M. ANDRÉ ESCOJIDO, Secrétaire permanent, Conseil Supérieur de la famille, Québec
M. PAUL FANIEL, Cité St-Michel
Mlle JEANNINE FILION, Directrice du service social, Hôpital Ste-Justine, Montréal
Mme H. FORTIER-LANDRY, Cap-de-la-Madeleine
Le rév. ALBERT GAGNON, Séminaire St-François, Cap-Rouge
Dr. MAX GARFINKLE, Director, Centre for Psychological Services, Montréal
Dr JEAN GAUDREAU, Coordonnateur des Services d'aide aux étudiants, Commission des écoles catholiques de Montréal
M. GUSTAVE GAUTHIER, Directeur de la Clinique d'Orthophonie, Hôpital Ste-Justine, Montréal
Mlle FRANÇOISE GIGNAC, École Cardinal Villeneuve Inc., Québec
Le rév. ALBINI GIROUARD, Directeur, Institut Dorea Inc., Huntingdon
Mlle JEANNINE GUINDON, Directrice du Centre d'orientation, Montréal
Mr. JAMES HEWITT, Commission des écoles catholiques de Québec, Québec
Mlle GERMAINE HUOT, Québec
M. ROGER JAUVIN, Director, Rehabilitation Service, Montréal
Dr BERNARD JEAN, Surintendent, Hôpital Ste-Anne, La Malbaie
Dr RAYMOND LAFONTAINE, Neurologue, Montréal
M. ANDRÉ LANDRY, Directeur, Services à l'enfance, Service social de Hull, Hull
M. PIERRE LAPLANTE, Directeur du conseil des œuvres, Montréal
Mme JULIENNE B. LAROSE, Outremont
M. LOUIS-MARIE LAVOIE, Directeur de l'Enseignement professionnel court, Commission des écoles catholiques de Québec
Dr DENIS LAZURE, Directeur du Département de psychiatrie infantile, Hôpital Ste-Justine, Montréal
M. PIERRE LECLERC, Fédération des loisirs du Québec
Mlle AIMÉE LEDUC, Montréal
Dr CLAUDE MAILHOT, Directeur général des Services à l'enfance, Ministère de la famille et du bien-être social, Québec
M. ROGER MARIER, Sous-ministre, Ministère de la famille et du bien-être social, Québec
M. ARMAND MARTEL, Secrétaire-conjoint, Conseil superieur de l'éducation, Québec
M. JEAN-MARIE MARTIN, Président du Conseil supérieur de l'éducation, Québec
Mrs. M. B. MCCRAE, Children's Service Centre, Montréal

Mme Berthe Michaud, Directrice du Service social scolaire, Commission des écoles catholiques de Montréal
M. Maurice Miron, Directeur du service social, commission scolaire, Régionale Lignery, Candiac
Dr Jean-Jacques Paquet, Coordonateur de l'Orthopédagogie, Commission des écoles catholiques, Montréal
M. Paul-Emile Parent, Directur général de l'Ecole Mont St-Antoine Inc., Montréal
Abbé Eucharisté Paulhus, Vice-doyen, Faculté des sciences de l'éducation, Université de Sherbrooke, Sherbrooke
Dr Cyrille Pomerleau, Médecin-chef, Unité Sanitaire, Lévis
Abbé Reynald Rivard, Institut psycho-social, Trois-Rivières
Mlle Pauline Roy, Commission scolaire de Sherbrooke, Sherbrooke
Dr Albert Royer, Professeur titulaire de pédiatrie et directeur du département, Université de Montréal
Dr Paul Savary, Ste-Foy
Mr. Howard Stutt, Director of Special Education, School Board Commission of Greater Montréal
Mme Madeleine Thibault, Services psychologiques, Commission scolaire régionale Papineau, Buckingham
Mlle Marie Tremblay, Conseil des œuvres, Montréal
Le rév. Antoine Tremblay, Petit séminaire de Chicoutimi, Chicoutimi
Mlle Marcelle Turcotte, Directrice du Service de l'enseignement préscolaire, Ministère de l'éducation Québec
M. Paul-Yvon Vertefeuille, Coordonnateur de l'Opération 55 à la Commission des écoles catholiques de Montréal
M. Romuald Voyer, Clinique médico-psychologique, Sherbrooke
Dr. Brian Wherret, Home Care Programme, Montreal Children's Hospital, Montréal
Mrs. Madeline Wilson, Montreal Children's Hospital, Montréal

Saskatchewan Delegates / Délégués de Saskatchewan

Professor John Paul, Provincial Chairman, Faculty of Education, University of Saskatchewan, Saskatoon
Professor Hester Kernen, Associate Professor in Public Health Nursing, University of Saskatchewan, Saskatoon
Mrs. H. R. Lane, Free-lance Writer, Moose Jaw
Dr. C. J. Lamarre, Department of Paediatrics, University of Saskatchewan, Saskatoon
John Mahon, Educational Psychologist Consultant, Department of Public Health, Regina
Dr. V. L. Matthews, Professor of Social and Preventive Medicine, University of Saskatchewan, Saskatoon
Dr. Stirling McDowell, Executive Assistant, Saskatchewan Teachers' Federation, Saskatoon
Miss Margaret Patillo, Director, Women's Service, University of Saskatchewan, Saskatoon

Dr. H. W. Savage, Associate Professor of Education, College of Education, University of Saskatchewan, Saskatoon
Mrs. C. Shulver, Saskatchewan Homemakers Association, Woodrow
Miss Vera Spencer, Nursing Consultant, Saskatchewan Department of Public Health, Regina
Dr. Alex Stephens, Director, MacNeill Clinic, Saskatoon
Mrs. A. B. Van Cleave, Saskatchewan Home and School Federation, Regina

Co-operating Organization Representatives / Délégués des organismes nationaux associés

Anglican Church of Canada
Miss Anne Davison, Anglican Church House, Toronto
Association canadienne-française d'éducation d'Ontario
Gaston Beaulieu, Toronto
Association of Junior Leagues of America
Miss Joan Walker, Halifax
Boy Scouts of Canada
P. J. Horan, Assistant Director of Program Services, Ottawa
Canadian Association for Adult Education
Dr. Alan Thomas, Toronto
Canadian Association of Occupational Therapists
Miss Anne Gaylard, Supervisor of Occupational Therapy, Montreal Children's Hospital
Canadian Association of Physical Education, Health, and Recreation
Professor Claude Bouchard, Dept. of Physical Education, Université Laval, Québec
Canadian Association for Retarded Children
Mrs. T. H. Dunn, Sillery
Canadian Association of Social Workers
J. A. Carmichael, Winnipeg
Mlle Berthe Michaud, Montréal
Canadian Council of Christians and Jews
The Rev. Richard Jones, Toronto
Canadian Council of Churches
Miss Ruth Tillman, C.G.I.T. Secretary, Toronto
The Rev. Kenneth S. Wills, Toronto
Canadian Dental Association
Dr Henri Hamel, Québec
Dr. Donald Rife, Toronto
Canadian Dietetic Association
Miss Barbara Broadfoot, Toronto
Miss Anne Y. Burns, Ottawa
Canadian Education Association
Émile Arteau, Catholic School Commission of Québec, Québec
Clare Routley, Executive Secretary, CEA, Toronto
Canadian Education Week Committee

Mrs. J. D. Taylor, Hamilton

CANADIAN GIRL GUIDES ASSOCIATION
Mrs. C. C. Muir, Toronto

CANADIAN HOME ECONOMICS ASSOCIATION
Miss Helen Deveraux, Macdonald College, Montréal
Miss Marjorie Harris, Macdonald Institute, Guelph

CANADIAN HOME AND SCHOOL AND PARENT-TEACHER FEDERATION
Mrs. Ward Hallman, New Glasgow
A. J. Sands, Shelburne

CANADIAN MEDICAL ASSOCIATION
Dr. Harry Medovy, Winnipeg Children's Hospital, Winnipeg

CANADIAN MENTAL HEALTH ASSOCIATION
Dr. J. D. Griffin, National Office, Toronto
Mrs. G. C. V. Hewson, Toronto

CANADIAN NATIONAL INSTITUTE FOR THE BLIND
Miss J. Farthing, Toronto

CANADIAN NURSES ASSOCIATION
Dr. H. K. Mussallem, Ottawa
Miss Esther Robertson, Ottawa

CANADIAN PAEDIATRICS SOCIETY
Dr. Charles Carrier, Québec
Dr. V. Marchessault, St. Lambert

CANADIAN PHYSIOTHERAPY ASSOCIATION
Mme G. Ajzenberg, Montréal
Miss Carol Morency, Montreal Children's Hospital

CANADIAN PSYCHIATRIC ASSOCIATION
Dr. J. D. Atcheson, Thistletown Hospital, Rexdale
Dr Denis Lazure, Montréal

CANADIAN PSYCHOLOGICAL ASSOCIATION
Dr. M. S. Rabinovitch, Department of Psychology, McGill University, Montréal

CANADIAN PUBLIC HEALTH ASSOCIATION
Dr Georgette Gelinas, Medical Officer of Health, St. Laurent
Dr. Jean F. Webb, Chief Maternal and Child Health Division, Department of National Health and Welfare, Ottawa

CANADIAN RED CROSS SOCIETY
Mlle Suzanne des Rivières, La société canadienne de la croix-rouge
Ralph E. Wendeborn, Toronto

CANADIAN REHABILITATION COUNCIL FOR THE DISABLED
Miss Margaret McGuinness, Toronto

CANADIAN SAVE THE CHILDREN FUND
Mrs. Jean Tory, Toronto
Miss Carrine M. Wilson, Ottawa

CANADIAN TEACHERS' FEDERATION
Dr. S. McDowell, Saskatchewan Teachers' Federation, Saskatoon

CANADIAN WELFARE COUNCIL
Raymond Doyle, Ottawa

CATHOLIC CHARITIES COUNCIL OF CANADA
Miss Ada Greenhill, Catholic Family Service, Ottawa

CATHOLIC WOMEN'S LEAGUE OF CANADA
  Mrs. Ward Markle, Willowdale
COLLEGE OF GENERAL PRACTICE
  Dr. Curtis Lowry, Sawyerville
COUNCIL FOR EXCEPTIONAL CHILDREN
  Miss Gertrude Fatt, Board of Education, Toronto
  Dr. L. P. Patterson, Mackay Centre for Deaf and Crippled Children, Montréal
INDIAN-ESKIMO ASSOCIATION OF CANADA
  Le rév. André Renaud, Faculty of Education, Saskatoon
NATIONAL COUNCIL OF JEWISH WOMEN
  Mrs. N. I. Zemans, Calgary
NATIONAL COUNCIL OF WOMEN
  Mrs. Saul Hayes, Montréal
PRESBYTERIAN CHURCH IN CANADA
  Miss Mabel Booth, Toronto
  Miss Helen Tetley, Toronto
THE SALVATION ARMY
  Major Frank Jennings, Montréal
  Brigadier J. Douglas Sharp, Toronto
UNITED CHURCH OF CANADA
  Miss Olive D. Sparling, Toronto
VANIER INSTITUTE ON THE FAMILY
  The Right Rev. E. S. Reed, Bishop of Ottawa
  Murray Ballantyne, Montréal
VICTORIAN ORDER OF NURSES
  Miss Alice Gage, Ste. Rose de Laval
  Miss Christine MacArthur, Ottawa
YOUNG MEN'S CHRISTIAN ASSOCIATION
  Ed Smee, Ottawa
YOUNG WOMEN'S CHRISTIAN ASSOCIATION
  Mrs. W. H. Whan, Toronto

The following co-operating organizations were not represented at the conference:

  Association canadienne des éducateurs de langue française
  Canadian Arthritis and Rheumatism Society
  Canadian Catholic Conference
  Canadian Citizenship Council
  Canadian Health Education Specialists Society
  Canadian Hearing Society
  Canadian Jewish Congress
  Canadian School Trustees' Association
  Canadian Young Judaea
  Canadian Youth Hostel Association
  Catholic Women's League of Canada
  Community Planning Association of Canada
  National UNICEF Committee
  Society of Obstetricians and Gynaecologists of Canada

DONORS

Abitibi Power and Paper Co. Ltd.
Gordon S. Adamson & Associates
Ahern Safe Co. Ltd.
Mr. R. P. Alger
Algoma Steel Corporation Ltd.
All-Canada Radio and Television Ltd.
Alliance Mutual Life Insurance Co.
Andras, Hatch & Hetherington Ltd.

Myer Bald Ltd.
Mr. St. Clair Balfour
Bank of Montreal
Bank of Nova Scotia
Banque Canadienne Nationale
La Banque Provinciale
Beaver Lumber Company Ltd.
Bedard-Gerard Limited
Mr. G. M. Bell
Bell Telephone Company of Canada, Montréal
Bell Telephone Company of Canada, Toronto
J. P. Bickell Foundation
Birks and Sons (Ontario) Ltd.
Bohemian Maid Brewing Co. Ltd.
Borger Bros. (1963) Ltd.
Mr. A. E. Boyd
Mr. M. G. Boulanger
Braithwaites Limited
Mr. A. E. Branca, Q.C.
British American Oil Company
British Columbia Forest Products Ltd.
Brooks Equipment Limited
Brown Bros. Agencies Limited
Burns Bros. & Denton Limited
Mr. G. Allan Burton

CFRB Limited
Calgary Brewing & Malting Co. Ltd.
Calgary *Herald*
Canada Life Assurance Company
Canada Permanent Mortgage Corporation
Canada Steamship Lines Limited
Canada Valve & Hydrant Co. Ltd.
Canadair Limited
Canadian Imperial Bank of Commerce
Canadian Bank Note Company Limited
Canadian Corporate Management Co. Ltd.
Canadian Indemnity Company
Canadian Kodak Co. Ltd.
Canadian Pacific Railway Company
Canadian Salt Co. Ltd.
Canadian Utilities Limited
Canadian Westinghouse Co. Ltd.
James B. Carter Limited
Catholic Charities Store
Mr. E. J. Chambers
Chemcell (1963) Limited
Christie Brown & Company
Coast Steel Fabricators Limited
Cockfield Brown & Co. Ltd.
Confederation Life Association
Consumers' Gas Company Ltd.
Continental Distributors Limited
Cowin Steel Co. Ltd.
The Harold Crabtree Foundation
Credit Foncier Franco-Canada
Crown Life Insurance Company

Dr. Paul David
Deloitte, Plender, Haskins & Sells
Mr. Basil Dean
Distillers Corporation Limited
Dominion Securities Corporation Limited
Dominion Foundries & Steel Company
Dominion Stores Limited
Dominion Tar & Chemical Company

Dow Brewery Limited
Dow Chemical of Canada Limited
Mr. John W. R. Drummond
Mrs. Jane H. Dunn
Duplate Canada Limited
Du Pont of Canada

The T. Eaton Company Limited
The *Edmonton Journal*
Equitable Securities Company

Fiberglass Canada Limited
Firestone Tire & Rubber Co. of Canada
Mr. Phillip Fisher
Foundation Finance & Holdings Ltd.
Mr. E. C. Fox
Messrs. Friedman, Lieberman & Newson
Charles E. Frosst & Company
Mr. John A. Fuller

W. J. Gage Limited
General Distributors Limited
General Foods Limited
Gerard-Parizeau Ltée
The Frank Gerstein Charitable Foundation
Global Life Insurance Company
Goodyear Tire & Rubber Co. of Canada Ltd.
Gordon MacKay & Co. Ltd.
Greater Winnipeg Gas Co.
Great-West Life Assurance Co.
Greenshields Incorporated
Grenache Incorporated

Mr. W. H. Hall
Harlequin Books Limited
Harris & Partners Ltd.
Mr. Robert Hartog
Mr. D. S. Harvie
Messrs. Hean, Wylie & Dixon
H. J. Heinz Co. of Canada Ltd.
Mr. B. M. Hoffmeister
Mr. St. Clair Holland
Home Oil Co. Ltd.
Hospital for Sick Children
Hudson's Bay Company
Household Finance Corporation of Canada
Mrs. Ellen Howard
Hudson's Bay Oil & Gas Co.

Imperial Oil Limited
Imperial Optical Co. Ltd.
Imperial Tobacco Co. of Canada
Industrial Acceptance Corporation Ltd.
Inland Cement Co. Ltd.
International Business Machines
International Harvester Co. of Canada Ltd.

Mr. M. L. Jennison
Jenkins Bros. Ltd.

The Leon & Thea Koerner Foundation
Mr. W. C. Koerner
Kraft Foods Limited

John Labatt Limited
Mr. Walter C. Laidlaw
Mrs. Gertrude Laing
Mr. B. E. Langfeldt
Rene T. Leclerc Inc.
A. C. Leslie & Co. Ltd.
Lever Bros. Ltd.
Levy Auto Parts Co. Ltd.
Libling, Michener & Association
Mr. A. J. Little
The London *Free Press*
London Life Insurance Company
Loram Limited

McCabe Grain Co. Ltd.
Messrs. McCuaig, McCuaig, Desrochers, Beckingham & McDonald
Dr. Mary McKenty
Mr. A. C. McKim
Macaulay, Nicolls, Maitland & Co. Ltd.
Mrs. Stuart MacKay
MacLean-Hunter Publishing Co. Ltd.
Manitoba Brewer's Association
Manufacturers Life Insurance Co.
Maple Leaf Mills Ltd.
Major General A. Bruce Matthews
Medicine Hat Brick & Tile Co.
Melchers Distilleries Limited

Molson Breweries Limited
Mr. John H. Molson
The Monarch Life Assurance Co.
Montreal Construction Supply & Equipment Co. Ltd.
Montreal Engineering Co. Ltd.
Montreal Trust Company
Morgan, Ostiguy & Hudon
Mr. R. E. Moore

National Trust Company Limited
Mr. A. D. Nesbitt
Nesbitt, Thomson & Co. Ltd.
The Nickle Foundation
North American Hide Corporation Alberta Limited
Northland Utilities Limited
Northwestern Utilities Limited

Mr. E. Orlando
O'Keefe Foundation
J. Rene Ouimet Limited

People's Credit Jewellers
Pepsi-Cola Canada Limited
Mrs. R. F. Phillips
Pigott Construction Co. Ltd.
Pitblado, Hoskins & Co.
Poole Construction Limited
La prévoyance compagnie d'assurances
Proctor & Gamble Co. of Canada Ltd.
Produits Alimentaires Catelli Ltée

Radio Saint Boniface Limited
Mr. W. McG. Rait
Lt. Col. Colin Rankin
The Reader's Digest Association
Mr. L. Remillard
Remington Rand Limited
James Richardson & Sons Ltd.
Messrs. Riddell, Stead, Graham & Hutchinson
Rolland Paper Co. Ltd.
The Royal Bank of Canada
The Royal Trust Company

Saan Stores Limited
Salada Foods Limited
E. L. Sauder Limited
Searle Grain Co. Ltd.
The Shawinigan Water and Power Co.
Shell Canada Limited
The Saul Silverman Family Foundation
Simard-Beaudry Inc.
Simpson-Sears Ltd.
Mr. D. R. Sinclair
Mr. James Smith
Société d'administration et de fiducie
Société nationale de fiducie
Southam Press Limited
R. James Speers Corporation Ltd.
St. Lawrence Sugar Refineries
Mr. George H. Steer, Q.C.
Steel Company of Canada Ltd.
J. Stevenson & Associates
Studebaker of Canada Ltd.
Sun Life Assurance Co. of Canada

Tele-Metropole Corporation
The Toronto-Dominion Bank
The *Toronto Star* Limited
Trust général du Canada
Turnbull Elevator Limited

Underwood Limited
Union Carbide Canada Limited
Union Electric Supply Co. Ltd.
Union Milk Co. Ltd.
United Auto Parts
United Management Limited

Mr. R. Howard Webster
Weldwood of Canada Limited
Western Manitoba Broadcasters Limited
Mr. Norman E. Whitmore
Mr. C. M. Willoughby
Winnipeg *Free Press*
Winnipeg Supply & Fuel Co. Ltd.
The Winnipeg *Tribune*
Wood, Gundy & Company
Wrights' Canadian Ropes Limited

Yarrows Limited

Government Participation

Grants were received from the Government of Canada through the Department of National Health and Welfare and the Welfare Grants Programme. The governments of the following provinces also supported the conference financially: Alberta, British Columbia, Manitoba, New Brunswick, Nova Scotia, Ontario, Prince Edward Island, and Québec.

Lightning Source UK Ltd.
Milton Keynes UK
UKHW010014210722
406167UK00002B/442